Excel

YEARS 7 to 8

Grammar and Punctuation Workbook

ESSENTIAL skills

Get the Results You Want!

PASCAL PRESS

Jane Baker

Reprinted 2016, 2017, 2020, 2021, 2022, 2023, 2024, 2025

ISBN 978 1 74125 411 2

Pascal Press
PO Box 250
Glebe NSW 2037
(02) 9198 1748
www.pascalpress.com.au

Publisher: Vivienne Joannou
Project editors: Mark Dixon and Leanne Poll
Edited by Leanne Howard
Series developer and consultant: Kristine Brown
Reviewed by Maya Puiu
Cover and page design by DiZign Pty Ltd
Typeset by lj Design (Julianne Billington)
Printed by Vivar Printing/Green Giant Press

Acknowledgements
The author and publisher would like to thank Carole Wilkinson for her permission to reprint an extract from Dragon Moon (Black Dog Books, Fitzroy, Vic., 2007).

Contents

To the student

This book has been specifically designed to teach you the essential grammar and punctuation terms, rules and conventions for the Year 7 and 8 Australian Curriculum English course. Knowing more about the grammar of English and about the way we use punctuation will help you develop into a good writer.

Each chapter has two sections: a grammar section and a punctuation section. Each section begins with a sample text and is followed by a boxed explanation of the grammar or punctuation points highlighted in the text.

When you read the explanation, look back to the sample text to understand how the grammar point or rule actually works in written language. The exercises that follow will help you practise your knowledge and apply that knowledge in your own writing.

Each chapter builds on the previous chapter, so when you are working don't be afraid to go back to a previous chapter to revise something you are not sure of.

There are four Revision Tests. The questions in these tests are in the style of NAPLAN Test questions. However, they do not cover every type of question you might get in the NAPLAN Tests. Their purpose is to revise and test the previous four chapters, and so they focus only on the content of these chapters. They will, however, give you practice in the content and structure of many NAPLAN questions.

Always work in good light and take your time. Don't rush, because that's how mistakes happen. With this book and practice, you will know more about the way English works and become a better writer. Good luck!

Jane Baker

UNIT ONE

A round blue world

Focus

Nouns; commas (1)

Grammar in use

Seventy-nine per cent of the Earth's **surface** is covered by **water**. That is why **astronauts** looked back from **space** in **surprise** and **delight** to see our planet, **Earth**, as a round blue world, a planet unlike any other in our solar **system**.

In the midst of all this water lie seven great continents: Australia, Asia, Europe, Africa, Antarctica, **North America** and South America. Smaller landmasses are scattered across the oceans. These are islands. They range in size from tiny coral cays to large masses of land like Greenland. The biggest island in the world is Australia. It is washed by the Pacific Ocean, the Indian Ocean and the **Great Southern Ocean**, as well as the waters of the **Torres Strait**.

Some countries, like **Japan** and New Zealand, are made up of several islands. Indonesia is unique in that it is an **archipelago**, a chain of 3000 islands running from west to east in the waters between Asia and northern Australia.

About grammar

Nouns name all the things that we speak or write about, that is, all the things in our world—people, places, things, creatures, feelings, ideas and qualities.

- **Common nouns**
  - name things in a general way; for example, **space**, **surprise**, **delight**.
  - name concrete things—things you can see or touch; for example, **surface**, **water**, **astronauts**. These are called **concrete nouns**.
  - name abstract things—things you can't see or touch, such as feelings or ideas; for example, **surprise**, **delight**, **system**. These are called **abstract nouns**.
  - name groups of things, living or not living; for example, a group of islands is an **archipelago**. These are called **collective nouns**. Other examples are *flocks* (of birds), *teams* (of players).
- **Proper nouns** name particular or specific things; for example, **Earth** (a particular planet) and **Japan** (a particular country). Proper nouns always start with a capital letter.
- Remember: if a proper noun consists of more than one word, every main word must be **capitalised**; for example, **North America**, **Great Southern Ocean**, **Torres Strait**. (We don't capitalise small words like *of* and *and*; for example, *Straits* **of** *Malacca*.)
- Nouns are either **singular** (for one thing) or **plural** (for more than one); for example, *astronaut* (singular) and *astronauts* (plural).

Boost your grammar skills

1 Read this information and underline every **noun**.

> Lakes are large bodies of water surrounded by land. In Australia, Lake Eyre is a dry salt lake that fills with runoff from heavy rains in Queensland. In Africa, Lake Victoria is a huge deep lake that supports fish, waterbirds, animals and people. The White Nile flows from this lake, joins the Blue Nile from Ethiopia, and so becomes the mighty Nile that reaches the Mediterranean Sea.

2 Write the **proper noun** from the list next to its matching **common noun**.

For example: island Iceland

Irishman   Eyre   Mexico   Kosciusko   Sahara   Amazon   French   Moscow

a lake ______________________ **b** river ______________________

c country ______________________ **d** language ______________________

e person ______________________ **f** mountain ______________________

g city ______________________ **h** desert ______________________

3 Read the text below and complete the following lists with **nouns** from that text.

> The catastrophic 1883 volcanic eruption on the island of Krakatoa in Indonesia sent an immense cloud of ash up into the atmosphere. As the island was torn apart by a series of mighty explosions, the sky filled with darkness. People thousands of miles away were filled with fear. In villages and on farms, flocks and herds ran about in fright and confusion.

Proper noun	Collective noun	Abstract noun

4 Write these **nouns** in the spaces, using the clues in brackets. The first one has been done for you.

world   fear   table   Juan Sebastian Delcano   globe   sailors   trepidation   edge

In ancient times (common) sailors went to sea in (abstract) ______________ and (abstract) ______________. They believed the (concrete) ______________ was flat like a (concrete) ______________ and that they would fall off its (concrete) ______________ if they travelled too far into unknown waters. In the sixteenth century Portuguese seamen, Ferdinand Magellan and (proper) ________ ______________ ______________, sailed right around the world proving that it is a (concrete) ______________, not a table.

5 Circle the type of **noun** underlined in each sentence.

For example: Curiosity drives most exploration. (concrete /(abstract))

a Magellan's ships were called *Trinidad*, *Santiago* and *Victoria*. (proper/concrete)

b In 1492 Admiral Zheng He of China sailed to India and beyond. (concrete/proper)

c Coral cays are built on the remains of dead corals. (concrete/collective)

d Sailors view storm clouds with anxiety. (abstract/concrete)

e Coral reefs are home to schools of bright fish. (proper/collective)

f The *Endeavour* was the name of Captain Cook's ship. (concrete/proper)

g Some islands are at risk of being swallowed by rising seas. (abstract/concrete)

h The crew greeted the sight of land with excitement. (abstract/concrete)

i Vikings were the first Europeans to reach America. (common/proper)

6 Tick (✔) the correctly labelled **nouns** and cross (✘) the incorrect ones. The first one has been done for you.

a Fairy penguins (proper noun ✘) come to Phillip Island (proper noun ✔) at dusk (abstract noun ✘).

b The highest mountain (proper noun) in Africa (common noun) is Kilimanjaro (proper noun).

c Undersea earthquakes (common noun) occur as frequently as land-based earthquakes (abstract noun).

d Lake water (concrete noun) in ancient volcanic craters (concrete noun) is noted for the beauty (abstract noun)

and variety of its colours (abstract noun).

7 Complete each sentence with a **noun** from the information in this chapter, using the clues in brackets. There may be more than one answer.

a ______________________ (proper) is a huge frozen landmass at the southern tip of the world.

b Penguins, walrus and (common) ______________________ live in the Great Southern Ocean.

c Tasmania was part of the (common) ______________________ of Australia until the sea flooded Bass Strait.

d The (abstract) ______________________ of being upturned by a whale disturbed the sleep of many an old-time sailor.

e At dusk a (collective) ______________________ of ibis headed west into the sunset.

Punctuation in use

The great rivers of our world like the **Nile, Amazon, Ganges, Yangtze, Rhine, Mekong, Mississippi and the Murray-Darling system** are the lifeblood of the lands through which they flow. As they flow to the sea **they enrich land, irrigate crops, keep stock alive and maintain orchards and farms.**

About punctuation

- **Commas** help us make our meaning clear by separating the different parts of a sentence. We use them in many different ways.
- One use of commas is to **separate items** in a list; for example, the **Nile, Amazon, Ganges, Yangtze, Rhine, Mekong, Mississippi and the Murray-Darling system.**
- We don't usually place a comma after the **second-last item in a list** (that is, before *and* or *or*), but may sometimes do so for extra clarity in a long sentence.
- Sometimes items in a list may include **two or more words**; for example, **they enrich land, irrigate crops, keep stock alive and maintain orchards and farms.**

Boost your punctuation skills

1 Add **commas** where necessary in the following sentences.

a The Rhine flows from Switzerland through France Germany Belgium and The Netherlands.

b Container ships bulk ore carriers oil tankers and ocean liners travel the high seas.

c The Paroo Warrego Namoi Bogan Macquarie and Castlereagh rivers all flow into the Darling River.

d Travelling south along the Nile you pass through the countries of Egypt North Sudan South Sudan and Uganda.

e Lake Baikal the Caspian Sea the Aral Sea and the Black Sea are all large inland stretches of water in Europe and Asia.

f Freight barges eel boats tourist ships and small rowing boats ply the waters of the Rhine.

g Ships on the Great Lakes of North America carry household goods wheat timber oil and machinery between cities.

2 Edit this student's recount in red pen for all missing **capital letters** and **commas**.

When we travelled to lake Eyre in south Australia we camped beside the water. We were woken the next morning by a great noise. The lake was covered with thousands of birds. There were pelicans ibis herons spoonbills and every kind of waterbird imaginable. My father was especially happy because he saw a banded stilt. My sister spied a freckled duck so she was happy too. On the long trip home we crossed over the northern Territory queensland and new south wales borders.

3 This student loves **commas** and uses far too many. Cross out all the unnecessary commas.

> The waters, of the Indian Ocean, wash the coasts of Australia, Indonesia, Thailand, India, Saudi Arabia, and all the countries, of Africa's east coast. They also surround islands, like the Maldives, Sri Lanka, and Madagascar.

4 Complete these sentences from information in this chapter and add **commas** where necessary. The first one has been done for you.

a Three of the great oceans of the world are the Great Southern Ocean, the Pacific Ocean, and the Indian Ocean.

b Some of the rivers that flow into the Darling River are

____

____

c Four large inland seas are

____

____

d Australian waterbirds include

____

____

e Some countries are islands, including

____

____

5 Insert the missing **capital letters** and **commas** in these sentences. Remember: all **proper nouns** need capital letters.

a The warm current off the coast of australia brings whales penguins and seals up to feed.

b The great barrier reef is home to corals eels rays shellfish sharks and myriads of fish.

c The todd river in alice springs is usually dry.

d Lake jindabyne is a man-made lake that is home to trout redfin eels and cod.

e Passage across a river can be gained via stepping stones a ford a causeway a fallen log a flying fox or a bridge.

f Caves beneath the ground are networks of narrow passageways chambers of various sizes and sudden drops into the darkness.

UNIT TWO

Living together

Focus

Pronouns; commas (2)

Grammar in use

Maria Leonello's vegetable patch was the best in the street and **she** knew it. Old Jones, with **his** tomatoes so carefully staked and tied, could not match **her** rich, ripe, red fruit. And as for the Napolis, **their** grape vine might be a marvel to behold, but her zucchinis matched **theirs** for size and bettered them for colour.

Maria hummed as **she** worked. 'People who love people ...,' she warbled just as I ambled past with my brother. We both snorted with laughter. Mrs Napoli, working in her garden next door to Maria, looked up and glared. The kookaburra in the tree above us raised his head and laughed.

About grammar

- **Pronouns** are words that stand in place of nouns. They help us avoid repeating nouns in a text; for example, *and* **she** *knew it* instead of *and Maria Leonello knew it.*
- **Personal pronouns** stand in place of nouns. The personal pronouns are *I, me, we, us,* (**first person**—the person speaking*)* *you,* (**second person**—the person spoken to) *he, him, she, her, it, they* and *them* (**third person**—the person spoken about).
- **Possessive pronouns** also stand for nouns but they show ownership; for example, **his** *tomatoes/***their** *grape vine/matched* **theirs** *for size.* The possessive pronouns are *my, mine, our, ours,* (first person) *your, yours,* (second person) *his, her, hers, its, their* and *theirs* (third person). (Strictly speaking *my, your, her, his, its, our* and *their* are **possessive adjectives**, but as they are sometimes called possessive pronouns we will call them that here.)
- All pronouns must **agree in number** with the noun they replace (either singular or plural); for example, *Maria hummed as* **she** *worked,* not *Maria hummed as* **they** *worked.*
- Remember: there are many other kinds of pronouns too; for example, *who, what, which, whose, this, that, these* and *those.*

Boost your grammar skills

1 Read this story extract and underline all the **personal pronouns** you can find.

From the far end of the pool came a scream followed by a splash. Taha didn't hesitate. He plunged straight in and headed for the deep end, his arms churning the water into froth. A little redheaded girl was struggling in the water. She stayed under longer each time she sank. The crowd roared its approval as Taha reached her and then, by rolling over onto his back, towed her to the wall of the pool and safety.

2 Edit this diary entry to make it more interesting by replacing the underlined nouns with **personal pronouns**. The first one has been done for you.

Joe, Kamal and the boys went down to the creek. Joe told Kamal and the boys them there were plenty of yellowbelly to be caught. Kamal threw in a line and soon Kamal ________________ felt something snatch at the line ________________. Scott yelled that Scott ________________ could see something on the end of Kamal's line. The line raced from the rod so fast Scott and Joe ________________ had to hold the rod steady as Kamal slowly reeled in the line. With a great spray of water an old man eel flipped onto the bank. The old man eel ________________ was all of two metres in length.

3 Circle the correct **personal pronoun**. Remember: pronouns must agree with their nouns in number.

For example: Katy is a kind girl so (he/she/it) has many friends.

a Friendship begins with small things. Saying hello to a new girl, sitting next to (him/her) in class or joining (them/her) for lunch can be the start of a long friendship. Sometimes (he/she/it) will last a lifetime.

b Mateship is part of being an Australian. If a mate is sad, you cheer (it/him) up. If he has lost (his/her/their) footy boots, you help him find (her/them/it) and if he is in trouble you stick up for (them/him).

c Shared activities and interests cement friendships. (It/They/We) help friends know each other better. (It/Them/They) also help friends learn patience and generosity.

4 Write the missing **possessive pronoun** using the space clues. The first one has been done for you.

a A mean person says, "That's mine," but a generous person says, "That's o u r s. Let's share."

b The referee ruled it was not our ball but _ _ _ _ _ _ (the other side's).

c That pen is yours but this one is his and that one is _ _ _ _ (Anne's).

d The visiting team's colours are red and black but _ _ _ _ (our team's) are red and white.

e "Excuse me, that's my compass you are using. This one is _ _ _ _ _."

5 Write an appropriate **pronoun** in the spaces.

Elise and Sally, friends since kindergarten, have been joined by a new friend in high school. ________________ name is Ana and ________________ comes from Samoa. The three girls are all in the same class. ________________ all share the same sports group and ________________ favourite sport is netball.

6 Rewrite this student's accident report and replace the incorrect **pronouns**.

> The boys were all playing tag on the basketball court. Peter tripped over and broke her arm. Eddie and their mate took Peter up to the sick bay. Jemal carried our bag because Peter was too hurt to carry them.

____

____

____

____

____

____

7 Write this text in the first person using **first-person pronouns** (*I, me, we, us, my, mine, our, ours*). The first one has been done for you.

> They all agreed to meet at eleven o'clock. They were to bring a picnic lunch, their towels and their suncream. They should all bring their mozzie repellent too. It was a great summer for all of them. Sun, surf, sand, beach cricket and friendship—what more could any of them want?

We all agreed to meet at eleven o'clock.

____

____

____

____

____

____

8 Tick (✔) sentences that use **pronouns** correctly. Cross (✘) the incorrect sentences.

a Will you all bring your own lunches? ____________________

b Is Simon usually responsible for its brother? ____________________

c Our cricket team has won its last three matches. ____________________

d Lifesavers risk their lives for others. ____________________

e Joy and Jim believe the experiment is theirs to conduct. ____________________

Punctuation in use

"Come here, Lucy."

Lucy quietly made her way to the front and was handed a test paper by Mr Elias**, the Maths teacher**. On her way back Isabella**, the girl in the second seat,** whispered something about borrowing a ruler. Lucy smiled and passed her a spare ruler.

"Pass it back when you're finished**, will you?**"

Then everyone settled down to do the test.

Mr Elias broke the silence. "Was that a whisper up the back**, I wonder?**"

About punctuation

Commas are often used to separate

- **extra information** about a noun—information that might be interesting but which can be taken out without affecting the sentence meaning; for example, *by Mr Elias*, **the Maths teacher**/*Isabella*, **the girl in the second seat,** *whispered something.*
- **question tags** such as *will you, isn't it*; for example, *Pass it back when you're finished,* **will you?**
- **ending comments** from the rest of the sentence, such as *I think, I suppose, I suggest, I wonder*; for example, *Was that a whisper up the back,* **I wonder?**
- **names of persons** spoken to from the rest of the sentence; for example, *Come here, Lucy.*
- Remember: we don't always need to use commas in this way in very short sentences, especially in imaginative or informal writing. Often we just have to judge for ourselves whether or not a comma is required—will it make the sentence clearer or won't it?

Boost your punctuation skills

1 Add the missing **comma(s)**.

For example: Mr Smith and Mr Ibrahim, the carpenters, have been friends since boyhood.

a Charlie and Dave fishing mates for years are out on Jervis Bay looking for bream.

b May I sit with you in the library Aziza?

c Omar's uncle a doctor was born in Cairo in Egypt.

d Uncle David Mum's brother is coming to visit at the weekend.

e Shut the window Michael. It's very windy don't you think?

2 This text contains seven **commas**. Circle the four commas that should not be there.

> Mrs Zanetti, and Mrs Markson, next door, neighbours, share the produce of their gardens. Zannetti hens, keep the Markson family in eggs and Markson tomatoes help to make the rich Zanetti tomato sauce. It's great for neighbours, to share the things they grow, I reckon.

3 Edit Suzy's diary entry and add the missing **commas**.

> Thirteen is really grown up I think. My friends Amy Alice and Joy agree. Do Mum and Dad think so too I wonder? They let us go ten pin bowling by ourselves this afternoon. I asked Mum later if she thought I was grown up now. She said I was getting there. Parents mothers in particular really are annoying sometimes aren't they? They never give you a straight answer.

4 Add the missing **commas** to these sentences. (Remember the rules for commas in lists from Chapter 1.)

a Greg Leo Andy and Louis play squash together every Friday.

b Have you lost your compass again Craig? You must have a hole in your backpack I think.

c Netball basketball soccer tennis and squash are the winter sport options.

d The Magpies the Under-14s were named Best and Fairest in the Interschool competition.

e Blue Sarg Crow and Tadpole were our nicknames in primary school.

f Marie will you play chess with me at lunchtime?

5 Whose words in this dialogue use **commas** correctly—Steve's or Safi's?

> Steve: Safi do you want to go skateboarding, this weekend?
>
> Safi: I have to mow the lawn and wash the car on Saturday morning.
>
> Steve: We could go, on Saturday afternoon. Our friends will probably be at the skate park then I think.
>
> Safi: I could ask Ahmad, my brother, to help me so we could finish cleaning the car quickly. He might help, I think.
>
> Steve: He could come skateboarding with us, too if he likes.

Answer: ______________________________

6 Read this piece of nonsense verse and put in the missing **commas**.

> It's not a comet a comb a candle or a cradle;
> it's not even a camel or a crystal candelabra.
> It looks more like a tadpole I think
> and has a tail like a cat but
> a comma's not furred and certainly can't swim—
> of that we are sure dear Harry my friend—
> so we'll go with an ink spin that
> splotted a dot and dribbled a squiggle
> and that's the lot—for a comma.

UNIT THREE

All creatures great and small

Focus

Verbs; commas (3)

Grammar in use

A panther **slinks** along a ledge towards the tree that shelters the monkey tribe. There **is** no moon. A bank of clouds **is** obscuring the stars. Tonight he **has** a real chance of dining well.

He **lifts** his paws carefully and sets them down gently. He is being very quiet. Monkeys **have** sharp ears. If a twig **snaps** or a leaf rustles they hear. The young panther left his mother two days ago. He ate a small bird twenty-four hours ago and nothing since so he **feels** very hungry. He needs to eat. He pauses to listen, then slinks even lower to the ground as he approaches the monkey tree. They are asleep and he **believes** he has a chance.

About grammar

- **Verbs** are extremely important words. They tell us what is happening in a sentence—basically, what the nouns and pronouns are doing.
- Many verbs tell us what the things named by the nouns are physically doing. These are **action verbs**; for example, *a panther* **slinks**/*he* **lifts** *his paws/a twig* **snaps**.
- Some verbs tell us what the nouns are thinking and feeling; for example, *he* **feels** *very hungry/he* **believes** *he has a chance.* These are **thinking and feeling verbs**.
- Other verbs tell us about the relationships between the nouns mentioned in the sentence. They are sometimes called **being** or **linking verbs**; for example, *There* **is** *no moon, Tonight he* **has** *a real chance.*
- Some verbs include a **helping** (or **auxiliary**) **verb**; for example, *A bank of clouds* **is** *obscuring the stars.* Common auxiliary verbs are *is, are, was, were, do, did, does, will, have, has, had, can, may, might, should, could* and *would.* When a verb is made of more than one word it is called a **verb group**.

Verbs

- change form to different **tenses** to show when things happen.
- in the **present tense** are talking about time now; for example, *shelters, rustles.*
- in the **past tense** are talking about time past; for example, *left, ate.*
- ending in **ing** show that the action is **continuous**; for example, *is obscuring.*
- must always **agree in number** with their nouns; for example, *Monkeys* **have** *sharp ears,* not *Monkeys* **has** *sharp ears.* (See Chapter 7 for more on verb tenses.)

Boost your grammar skills

1 Underline the **action verb** and circle the noun that does the action.

- **a** The old gorilla beat his chest.
- **b** Eleven mountain goats were leaping through the rocks.
- **c** Jaguars, a nocturnal species, hunt by night.
- **d** With a squeak of alarm, the meerkat fled down her burrow.
- **e** A snake, unnoticed by his prey, slid silently towards the rabbit.

2 Circle the correct form of the **being verb** in each of the following. Be sure it agrees in number with the **noun** it relates to.

- **a** The wolf (am/is/are) native to the Northern Hemisphere.
- **b** Gorillas (is/are) basking in the sunlight.
- **c** Wombats (are/is) cousins of koalas.
- **d** A moray eel (is/are) a predator among coral reefs.
- **e** The pelicans (was/were) at rest on the lake yesterday.

3 Write the appropriate **helping (auxiliary) verb** in the gaps to complete the verb groups.

have	do	have	would	will	has

- **a** Kestrels hovered in hope that a field mouse ______________ pop his head up in the grass.
- **b** Wild creatures ______________ attack only if they are threatened.
- **c** An orb spider ______________ spun a web in that shrub.
- **d** Yesterday the gazelles were hunted by a cheetah so today they ______________ moved on.
- **e** It is now daylight so all sensible wombats should ______________ gone underground to sleep.
- **f** Many animals ______________ not have the ability to distinguish one colour from another.

4 Write an appropriate **verb** from the list in each space. Be sure it agrees in number with its **noun**.

are	stay	look	sounds	feels	looks	is

- **a** The dingo's cry, heard on the cold night air, ______________ mournful indeed.
- **b** Wombat hair ______________ coarse while wallaby hair ______________ soft to the touch.
- **c** Snakes and lizards ______________ asleep all winter.
- **d** Lace monitor lizards ______________ ferocious but they ______________ really very shy.
- **e** That owl ______________ sleepy but he's just thinking.

5 Complete the **tense** pattern for these **verbs**. The first one has been done for you.

Present	Simple past	Future	Continuous present	Continuous past
hiss	hissed	will hiss	is hissing	was hissing
stalk			is stalking	
	hibernated	will hibernate		
prey				
			is howling	

6 Change the underlined **verbs** to show **continuous action**. Keep the same general **tense** (present, past or future). The first one has been done for you.

a Brolgas **dance** in the grass by the lagoon. are dancing

b A lyrebird **imitates** the sound of a camera shutter closing. ______________

c The brown snake **sunned** himself on a warm rock. ______________

d Five fairy wrens **flitted** through the scrub. ______________

e The grey nurse shark **cruises** just offshore. ______________

7 Underline all the **verbs** in the **past tense**. Most, but not all, end in *ed*.

> Patch was a tiny ball of fluff when a cyclist found him in the dust by the roadside. The little ringtail was so small the cyclist buttoned him into his shirt pocket and ferried him to a wildlife carer who was happy to care for the little orphan. She made him a little nest and fed him native flowers and fruit until he grew into handsome adult. Then she returned him to the Australian bush.

8 Elizabeth has mixed up her **tenses**. Cross out the errors and write the corrections.

> Last night I heard a loud huff and hiss outside my window. I looks out and there is a large brushtail possum sitting on a branch staring at me. He has bright black eyes. His little button nose was pink and he is holding one of Mum's roses in paws that looked just like little dark hands. He was very handsome but when he hissed loudly at another possum I think he sounds as if he could be quite cross.

____

____

____

____

____

Punctuation in use

Generally speaking, wombat mothers and babies share the same burrow and live together until the young one is ready to leave home. **Some mothers, however,** are soft-hearted. They leave home instead and allow the juvenile wombat to occupy the family burrow. **Wow,** what spoiled animals. I can just hear a baby wombat pleading, "Mum, **please,** I want to stay home. Please, please."

About punctuation

Commas are used to separate

- **connecting words and expressions** like *however, nevertheless, in fact, similarly* and *on the other hand* used at the start of a sentence; for example, **Generally speaking**, *wombat* ... (These words are called **connectives** because they connect the ideas between sentences.)
- **connectives** inserted in the middle of the sentence; for example, **Some mothers, however,** *are soft-hearted.* Note: the commas must go both before and after the inserted connective.
- **short expressions** like *wow, um, you know, gosh, good heavens* and *please* from the rest of the sentence; for example, **Wow**, *what spoiled animals*/*Mum*, **please**, *I want to stay home.*
- Remember: we use commas in many different ways but always with the purpose of **making our meaning clearer**.
- Note: a comma might **not** be needed in this way in very short sentences or in informal texts.

Boost your punctuation skills

1 Put **commas** where needed.

For example: Regrettably, we have to admit that many species are now extinct.

a Unfortunately we have not seen a night parrot for several decades in Australia.

b Look there's a microbat flying past the old kurrajong tree.

c It's raining. Nevertheless the seagulls are still scavenging on the beach.

d South America's boa constrictor can in fact crush and swallow a full-grown pig.

e Sadly the bandicoots of Sydney are now found only in two small areas.

f Unbelievably lyrebirds can mimic both a chainsaw and a fire siren.

g Butterflies as a general rule sleep with wings upright while moths sleep with folded wings.

2 Put **commas** after expressions of surprise or attention-getting expressions.

For example: Goodness me, where will that pigeon roost next!

- **a** Quickly close the gate before the cattle get out.
- **b** Look that's an orb spider building its three-dimensional web.
- **c** Gosh see this! The peacock's showing off his fan feathers.
- **d** Hey look at this! The bees are swarming.
- **e** Heavens above what will that dolphin do next?

3 Cross out the mistakes and add **commas** where necessary in these sentences.

- **a** Hopefully there will be no mouse plague, this summer.
- **b** The cane, toad unhappily has been a disaster, for Australian wildlife.
- **c** Saltwater crocodiles, in fact have remained, almost unchanged, since the age of the dinosaurs.
- **d** Feral cats unexpectedly go back to their wild size as well as their wild habits.
- **e** Tragically New Zealand's moa was hunted, to extinction, in the nineteenth century.

4 Mark the three sentences that are incorrectly punctuated with a cross (✗). Remember the **comma** rules from the previous chapters.

- **a** ______ Big-footed kangaroos, wallabies and wallaroos are all, in fact, called *macropods.*
- **b** ______ Eagles build large untidy nests on cliff faces in the top of dead trees and sometimes even on tall buildings.
- **c** ______ Please, if you value our wild creatures, drive carefully at night.
- **d** ______ Barney the wildlife ranger runs regular night-spotting tours of the National Park.
- **e** ______ The blue whale the biggest animal in the world eats the tiniest creature krill.

5 This report was written in a hurry. Improve it by putting in all the missing **commas**.

> Meerkats like penguins live in colonies. They share multiple burrows and unusually take turns in looking after their young. Routinely they set one meerkat to watch for danger some to clean the burrows and others to hunt for food. Nevertheless every meerkat stays on the alert for danger. Babysitters carefully mind the colony's young and keep a wary eye out for danger.

6 Tick (✓) sentences that use **commas** correctly. Cross (✗) those that don't.

- **a** Listen I think, I can hear a whipbird. ______________
- **b** Wombats are not mute. In fact, they can squeal and hiss. ______________
- **c** Ringtailed possums, amazingly, can carry four babies on their backs. ______________
- **d** Dollarbirds, unbelievably fly to Australia, every summer from PNG. ______________

UNIT FOUR

How it all works

Focus

Sentences and verbs; capital letters

Grammar in use

Imagine a world without gravity. **Everything floats. Houses drift into space. Trees pull up their roots and lift into the sky.** People hover **in the air forever**.

Gravity holds our feet on the ground. Gravity carries **a dropped pencil** to the floor. It even draws a tiny, almost weightless, feather to the earth. **All planets have their own gravitational pull but space itself has no gravity.** Feathers and pencils float in space.

Astronauts float in space too. They must tie themselves to their spacecraft for work outside. They anchor their toolboxes too. Leave a **toolbox** loose and **it** will float away. No-one can bring it back. It becomes **another piece of space junk**.

About grammar

A **sentence**

- is a group of words that makes sense by itself. It always contains a **verb**; for example, *Everything* **floats**. *Houses* **drift** *into space.*
- usually has a **subject** (the noun that does the action); for example, **Everything** *floats.* **Houses** *drift into space.* However, sometimes they do not have a subject; for example, **Imagine** *a world without gravity.* Here the subject is unwritten—**you** *imagine …*
- usually also has a **predicate** (the rest of the sentence telling us about the subject); for example, *Houses drift* **into space**./*People hover* **in the air forever**.
- with one verb is a **simple sentence**. Most of the sentences in the text above are simple sentences.

The **predicate** can include an **object** (the noun that the verb acts upon); for example, *Gravity carries* **a dropped pencil** *to the floor.* However, sometimes it does not; for example, **Everything floats**.

We can join two or more simple sentences together to make a **compound sentence**; for example, **All planets have their own gravitational pull but space itself has no gravity**. We make compound sentences using conjunctions (joining words) such as *and*, *but*, *or*, *yet*, *so* and *then*.

In a compound sentence the subject of the second sentence can be:

- **left out**; for example, **Trees pull up their roots and lift into the sky** (second *trees* left out).
- **replaced by a pronoun**; for example, *Leave a* **toolbox** *loose and* **it** *will float away.*

(See Chapter 11 for more on compound sentences.)

When a written sentence is incomplete we call it a **sentence fragment**; for example, **another piece of space junk** (by itself, this is not a sentence—it is a fragment).

(See Chapter 15 for more on fragments.)

Boost your grammar skills

1 Circle all the **verbs**. Remember: some verbs can have more than one word (a verb group).

For example: Spilt coffee (was floating) like a puddle in space.

a Ocean tides rise and fall according to the moon's gravitational pull.

b Weightlessness in space can waste an astronaut's muscles.

c Astronauts were repairing a loose surface tile when they dropped a spanner into space.

d Those space engineers are wearing very heavy boots so they don't float away.

e Space junk often becomes a hazard for spacecraft.

2 Write the appropriate **subject** in the gap. The first one has been done for you.

A dust storm	The tremors	Glowing lava flows	Heavy surf	A mountain spring

a ______Heavy surf______ pounded the beach.

b ____________________ bubbled down the side of the gully.

c ____________________ rolled in thick and dark from the west.

d ____________________ smoked as they slid down the crater slope.

e ____________________ were felt far from the earthquake's epicentre.

3 Arrange these words to make a complete **simple sentence** and add punctuation.

For example: the two has world hemispheres The world has two hemispheres.

a catch the mountains rainfall sea from the ____________________

b floods land the enrich ____________________

c fill rivers Lake Eyre South Australia's ____________________

d lines earthquakes on most fault occur ____________________

4 Write an appropriate **verb** from the list to link the **subjects** and **objects** in these **sentences**.

flood	cause	bring	chills	bury

a Winter frost ____________________ noses and ears.

b Heavy rains ____________________ rivers and creeks.

c Tornadoes ____________________ great damage in the United States.

d Avalanches ____________________ whole villages and towns.

e Desert winds ____________________ dust storms to Beijing.

5 Write *S* for **simple sentence** and C for **compound sentence** for each of the following.

For example: Snow is beautiful but it is miserably cold. __C__

a Great wind cells move about the earth and these drive our weather. ____

b Monsoon winds bring the rainy season to the Tropics. ____

c Hot dry winds from Central Australia carry dust storms eastwards. ____

d A southerly buster refreshed Sydney but, at the same time, it dumped hail and damaged many roofs. ____

e It is raining in Queensland and soon Lake Eyre will fill. ____

6 Join each pair of **simple sentences** with *or, and, so* or *but*.

For example: The sun is bright. It is still cold. The sun is bright but it is still cold.

a The Earth revolves around the sun. At the same time it revolves on its own axis.

____

____

____

b Solar power is safe. Some places do not have enough sunshine for solar energy.

____

____

____

c The wind is picking up. It must be going to rain.

____

____

____

d We must take shelter. The storm will overtake us.

____

____

e Don't stand under trees in a storm. Lightning might strike you.

____

____

f We live every day with the sun right above us. Most of us know very little about it.

____

____

____

7 Cross (✗) the options that are **sentence fragments**.

a Galaxies full of billions of stars. ____

b Having examined it by telescope. ____

c The correct name for a falling star is a meteor. ____

d An eerie green light appeared before the storm. ____

e A beautiful red sunset warm and glowing. ____

8 Underline the incomplete **sentences**.

> Watching the sky. A black and purple storm approached. Peter saw jagged lightning on the horizon. A strange green light. A scurry of leaves. It was raining.

Punctuation in use

Thousands of years ago, Persia, the country we now know as **Iran**, had air conditioning. It was provided by the wind. Towers rose into the air from buildings high enough to catch the hot desert wind through an opening on the windward side. **Egypt** and other countries in the **Middle East** had similar cooling systems. The wind funnelled down the tower to a canal dug deep under the buildings where soil temperature is always cool. From there it dispersed through buildings as a cool and refreshing breeze.

About punctuation

- We use **capital letters** to begin every sentence and full stops to end all sentences that are statements (i.e. they do not ask a question).
- All **proper nouns** begin with capital letters; for example, **I***ran*, **E***gypt*, **M***iddle* **E***ast*.
- Capital letters start names, titles, months, days of the week, organisations, institutions, brand names, religions, languages, nationalities and important festivals.
- Remember: **all main words** in the proper noun need capital letters; for example, **M***iddle* **E***ast*, not *middle East* or *Middle east*. However, we don't use capitals for little words like *and*, *of*, *in* and *the* unless they come first in the title.
- Sometimes modern brand names do **not** use capital letters in order to get attention; for example, *adidas*, *intel* and *citibank*.
- Note: many words may be **common nouns** (no capitals) in some sentences and **proper nouns** in others; for example, *They saw* **C***aptain Martin standing on the deck* but *The* **c***aptain was the last to leave his ship.*

Boost your punctuation skills

1 Write the names of these institutions and organisations correctly using **capital letters** where necessary.

- **a** the united nations ______
- **b** the international red cross ______
- **c** the world wildlife fund ______
- **d** taronga park zoo ______
- **e** keep australia beautiful ______
- **f** friends of the earth ______

2 Rewrite these book and film names using correct **capitalisation**.

- **a** *the sorcerer's apprentice* ______
- **b** *the fellowship of the ring* ______
- **c** *a midsummer night's dream* ______
- **d** *the obernewtyn chronicles* ______
- **e** *pride and prejudice* ______
- **f** *harry potter and the deathly hallows* ______

3 Read the following sentences and write down any words that need a **capital letter**.

a chernobyl and fukushima are the sites of the world's worst nuclear accidents.

____

b urumchi, in china, is powered by electricity generated by wind and water.

____

c the international space station orbits about 350 kilometres above earth.

____

d iron ore is mined in the kimberley Ranges of western Australia.

____

e the three gorges dam in china is the biggest hydroelectric dam in the world.

____

4 Underline any word that is missing its **capital letter** in these sentences about world religions.

a christmas occurs on december 25 and remembers the birth of jesus.

b diwali, a hindu celebration, is also called the festival of lights.

c hannukkah is a jewish festival that is also called a festival of lights.

d eid il fitr is a muslim celebration to mark the end of the ramadan fast.

e the sacred book of Buddhism is called the tripitaka.

5 Add missing **capital letters** to this rhyme that helps us remember the days in every month.

thirty days hath september,
april, june and november.
all the rest have thirty-one
save february alone
which has twenty-eight days clear
and twenty-nine each leap year.

6 Add any missing **capital letters** to the titles and names of these people.

a reverend Charles Turner

b his royal Highness, king jigme wanchuk of bhutan

c governor general of australia

d captain fogarty fegan of hmas jervis bay

e emperor napoleon of France

f Ben Chifley, prime minister of australia

7 Write a **capital letter** or a small letter as necessary in the gaps of this text.

___ailing ship captains knew to sail ___outh from the ___quator until they reached the ___reat ___outhern ___cean. ___ere they could catch the trade winds that would carry them east until they reached the ___acific ___cean. ___he only problem was sailing through the stormy ___ass ___trait between the mainland of Australia and ___asmania. ___ragically, many ___hips have perished in those treacherous ___eas.

Revision Test 1

Grammar

Shade one circle to show the correct answer.

1 Which line contains only nouns?

- ◯ deep, shallow, high, wide, long
- ◯ seal, shark, fish, crab, whale
- ◯ fall, chatter, leap, sing, climb
- ◯ sing, alone, crawl, scale, lamp

2 Which circled word in this sentence is a noun?

Then the horse bolted from the stable.

- ◯ then
- ◯ stable
- ◯ bolted

3 Which word is a proper noun?

- ◯ ship
- ◯ river
- ◯ ocean
- ◯ Sydney

4 Which underlined noun needs a capital letter?

Apples, pears and potatoes grow well in tasmania.

◯ ◯ ◯

5 Which word is a concrete noun?

- ◯ happiness
- ◯ chair
- ◯ loneliness
- ◯ fear
- ◯ wonder

6 Which underlined word is a concrete noun?

The removalists loaded the tables into the truck with care.

◯ ◯ ◯

7 Which word is an abstract noun?

- ◯ ice
- ◯ rain
- ◯ snow
- ◯ anxiety

8 Which word is **not** an abstract noun?

- ◯ picture
- ◯ gloom
- ◯ sadness
- ◯ strength

9 What kind of noun belongs in the space?

The ________________ chased the thief down the street.

- ◯ concrete noun
- ◯ abstract noun

10 Which word is a collective noun?

- ◯ basket
- ◯ cattle
- ◯ flock
- ◯ shoes

11 Which line contains only collective nouns?

- ◯ fear, wallaby, mountain, mob
- ◯ shoes, basket, flock, cattle
- ◯ star, explorer, galaxy, gas
- ◯ herd, fleet, team, crew

12 Which word is **not** a collective noun?

- ◯ shoal
- ◯ mob
- ◯ herd
- ◯ buffaloes

13 Which word is a personal pronoun?

- ◯ if
- ◯ am
- ◯ is
- ◯ we

14 Which circled word is a possessive pronoun?

Mrs Meadows planted (roses) in (her) front (garden).

- ◯ roses
- ◯ her
- ◯ garden

In questions 15–17, which pronoun correctly completes the sentence?

15 That's the book ____________________ gave me.

- ◯ us
- ◯ she
- ◯ mine
- ◯ our
- ◯ me

16 The platypus mother lays ____________________ eggs in a river bank tunnel.

- ◯ our
- ◯ his
- ◯ her
- ◯ their

17 Most animals claim one piece of territory as ____________________.

- ◯ mine
- ◯ theirs
- ◯ ours
- ◯ yours

18 Which line contains only verbs?

- ◯ travel, exploration, darkness, flight
- ◯ deep, constellation, explode, was
- ◯ swim, investigate, descend, dive
- ◯ friend, mateship, forgive, laughter

19 Which circled word is a verb?

Paul (is) over (there) by the (wattle tree).

- ◯ is
- ◯ wattle tree
- ◯ there

20 Which underlined word group makes a complete verb?

Which of (you two) boys (will carry) the (cricket gear) back to the shed?

- ◯ you two
- ◯ will carry
- ◯ cricket gear

21 Which circled word is a helping verb in this sentence?

The boys (are) playing football on the oval (behind) the (school).

- ◯ are playing
- ◯ behind
- ◯ school

22 Which sentence is correct?

- ◯ The choir is singing in four-part harmony yesterday.
- ◯ The choir are singing in four-part harmony yesterday.
- ◯ The choir sang in four-part harmony yesterday.

23
- ◯ All the students are on holidays.
- ◯ All the students is on holidays.

In questions 24–25, which option is a sentence?

24
- ◯ Riley and Sam skiing this weekend.
- ◯ Riley and Sam going skiing this weekend.
- ◯ Riley and Sam this weekend.
- ◯ Riley and Sam are going skiing this weekend.

25
- ◯ Maria and her friends enjoy bird watching in the National Park.
- ◯ Maria watching in the National Park.
- ◯ Maria and her friends.
- ◯ Maria and her friends bird watching in the National Park.

Punctuation

In questions 1–2, where should the missing comma go?

1 The meal was a plate ○ of rice ○ beans and ○ fish.

2 Generally ○ speaking ○ owls are not seen ○ during the day.

In questions 3–8, which sentence is correctly punctuated?

3
- ○ Wow, see how red Mars, looks tonight.
- ○ Wow, see how red Mars looks tonight.

4
- ○ The campers each carried a tent water food and a hat.
- ○ The campers each carried a tent, water, food and a hat.
- ○ The campers each carried a tent, water, food, and a hat.
- ○ The campers each, carried a tent, water, food, and a hat.

5
- ○ Samantha will you show Isaac where the library is please.
- ○ Samantha will you show Isaac where the library is, please.
- ○ Samantha, will you show Isaac, where the library is, please.
- ○ Samantha, will you show Isaac where the library is, please.

6
- ○ The crocodile, native to north Australia, is considered a living dinosaur.
- ○ The crocodile native to north Australia, is considered a living dinosaur.

7
- ○ He piled grass and twigs lit a match and blew hard to encourage a flame.
- ○ He piled grass, and twigs lit a match and blew hard to encourage a flame.
- ○ He piled grass and twigs, lit a match and blew hard to encourage a flame.
- ○ he piled grass and twigs lit a match and blew hard to encourage a flame.

8
- ○ Lisa goes to netball on Saturdays unless of course it is raining.
- ○ Lisa goes to netball on Saturdays unless, of course, it is raining.
- ○ Lisa goes to netball on Saturdays, unless of course, it is raining.
- ○ Lisa goes to netball on Saturdays unless of course, it is raining.

9 Which sentence has all its capital letters in the right place?
- ○ New Zealand's Mount Tarawera volcano exploded in 1886.
- ○ New Zealand's mount tarawera volcano exploded in 1886
- ○ New zealand's Mount Tarawera volcano exploded in 1886.
- ○ new Zealand's Mount tarawera volcano exploded in 1886.

In questions 10–13, which sentence is correctly punctuated?

10
- ◯ koalas and wombats are first cousins
- ◯ Koalas and wombats are first cousins.
- ◯ Koalas and Wombats are first cousins.
- ◯ koalas and wombats are first cousins.

11
- ◯ Joern Utzon, a Danish architect designed the Sydney Opera House.
- ◯ Joern Utzon, a Danish architect, designed the Sydney Opera House.
- ◯ Joern Utzon a Danish architect, designed the Sydney Opera House
- ◯ Joern Utzon, a Danish architect, designed the Sydney Opera House,

12
- ◯ The tropic of Capricorn runs through Queensland.
- ◯ the Tropic of Capricorn runs through Queensland
- ◯ The Tropic of Capricorn runs through Queensland
- ◯ the tropic of capricorn runs through Queensland

13
- ◯ The black box is an australian invention.
- ◯ The Black Box is an australian invention.
- ◯ The black box is an Australian invention.
- ◯ The Black Box is an Australian invention.

14 Which word should start with a capital letter?
- ◯ month
- ◯ decade
- ◯ century
- ◯ year
- ◯ april
- ◯ millennium

15 Which title is correctly punctuated?
- ◯ sir charles Kingsford Smith
- ◯ Sir Charles Kingsford Smith
- ◯ Sir charles Kingsford Smith
- ◯ Sir Charles kingsford Smith

UNIT FIVE

First people

Focus
Prepositions and phrases; end punctuation

Grammar in use

'First people' is the name given **to** the original inhabitants of any land.

Generally speaking, indigenous people have not been treated well **by** newcomers to their lands. For example, the Iceni **of Britain** were all but wiped out **by the Romans**.

Indigenous Australians, having no resistance **to** foreign diseases, suffered terribly when Europeans arrived. Measles killed hundreds **within months**. Accustomed to free range hunting, Aboriginal people also suffered because of the European need for cropping and grazing land. The land was their source **of food and shelter**. It was also their spiritual home. The loss of their land was a source of great anguish to them.

About grammar

Prepositions

- are words like *to, of, by, within, for, in, with, on, towards, after, beside, along, around, from, under, above, into, inside* and *beyond.*
- are used before nouns to make **prepositional phrases**; for example, **to** *the original inhabitants*/**by** *newcomers*/**to** *foreign diseases.* These phrases add detail about the nouns or verbs in a sentence.

A prepositional phrase

- can tell us more about a **verb** (when, where, how, why, to what extent, and so on); for example, *wiped out* **by the Romans**/*killed hundreds* **within months**.
- can also tell us more about a **noun** or **pronoun**; for example, *Iceni* **of Britain**/*source* **of food and shelter**.
- Remember: take care to place a prepositional phrase **as near as possible** to the noun or verb it gives details about. Look at the difference in meaning between these two sentences: *The people* **in the south** *lived for only a short time.*
  The people lived for only a short time **in the south**.

Boost your grammar skills

1 Write *S* for **sentence** or *P* for **phrase** for each of the following.

a The Gadigal people are the first people of the Sydney basin. ____

b in the Blue Mountains region ____

c The land of the Wiradjuri people lies west of the Blue Mountains. ____

d around the shores of Botany Bay ____

e Shellfish, eels and fish were trapped or speared. ____

2 Underline any **prepositional phrases** in these sentences. There may be more than one in each sentence.

a Some rock paintings in the West Australian Kimberleys are millennia old.

b Yagan was a warrior who lived and fought for his land in Western Australia.

c Rock paintings in the bush around Sydney depict the traditional life of local people.

d The poet, Oodgeroo Noonuccal, lived for most of her life on Stradbroke Island.

e It is difficult to survive in the arid western desert districts of Australia.

3 Write the appropriate **prepositional phrases** in the gaps. The first one has been done for you.

on his people's land	from the bush
in their old way	of the Bunuba people
in the hearts	for three years
from the ground	a fearless Aboriginal warrior

Jandamarra, a fearless Aboriginal warrior, decided he would not allow Europeans to take over his people's land in the Kimberleys as had happened down south. Here, ______________________, he took a stand against the continuing land hunger of the white man. ______________________, he carried on his fight to prevent his land, the land ______________________, being cleared for cattle grazing. Without their land his people could not live ______________________ by hunting, fishing and gathering roots ______________________ and berries ______________________. Jandamarra was killed in his war but his memory lives on ______________________ of his people.

4 Circle the **verb** that the underlined **prepositional phrase** tells us about. The first one has been done for you.

a Bennelong of the Eora people (travelled) across the seas to England in 1792.

b Gurrumul Yunupingu played in a band before going out on his own.

c Emily Kyngwarrye painted for many years in the desert regions of Central Australia.

d Neville Bonner, the first Aboriginal parliamentarian, was elected to the Australian Senate.

e In 1972 Wave Hill Station was recognised by the government of Australia as the traditional land of the Gurindji people.

f An Indigenous Australian cricket team toured England in the nineteenth century.

g Yvonne Goolagong played tennis around the world.

h Lionel Rose was a successful boxer in Australia and overseas.

5 Circle the **nouns** that the underlined **prepositional phrases** tell us about. The first one has been done for you.

- **a** The (Anungu Pitjantjatjara) of South Australia are the custodians of Uluru.
- **b** Reading the signs of animal movement in the bush is a traditional First People's skill.
- **c** Mum Shirl was known throughout NSW for her work on prisoners' behalf.
- **d** Australia's Aboriginal stockmen have an unequalled reputation for horsemanship.
- **e** People around the world have bought the paintings of Clifford Tjapaltjara.

6 Each sentence below is missing the **prepositional phrase** on its right. Mark the best place to put each phrase with a cross (✘). The first one has been done for you. There may be more than one possible position.

a Mountain people wore possum fur clothing. ✘	for warmth
b Aborigines used to set stone traps to catch eels.	in rivers
c Inuit can build houses in one or two hours.	out of blocks of ice
d Cathy Freeman ran in two Olympic Games.	for Australia
e Many ancient sketches have been found in desert regions.	on cave walls
f Storytelling is a feature of every race and culture.	by elders

7 Underline all the **prepositional phrases** in Mark's account of his attempt to catch a fish with a spear. You may find some phrases side by side.

> When we visited our cousins in the Northern Territory, they took us to a long sandy beach where two men with long spears were spearing fish. It looked easy, so I found a long thin branch and carefully whittled a stabbing point with my pocketknife.
>
> I waded in and looked about for a fish but I couldn't see one. Meanwhile, the Aboriginal men had already caught five by my count. Finally, a small fish flashed past my knee. I hurled my spear and plunged into the water to retrieve my catch. But there was no fish and my spear bobbed lazily on the surface.
>
> Just then a brown arm scooped me out of the water. 'Didn't you see that croc eyeing you off for dinner, little mate?' The tall man grinned as he pointed to the telltale swish of a croc tail in the water. 'Come away from the water and I'll show you how to make a real throwing spear while we wait till he goes away.'

8 Leah has underlined **prepositional phrases** in this text. Not all are correct. Circle the groups of words that are not phrases.

The Aboriginal flag is two bands of colour, red and black, with a round gold sun in the middle of the banner.

Punctuation in use

From: Sammy Smith
Subject: Hello!
Date: 2nd January
To: Gran <challoyd@firstnet.com.au>

Dear Gran, **Wow! I can't believe it**. You're finally on the internet. **What a cool grandma you are!** I told you it was easy, didn't I? Are you looking forward to having us stay next month? **I can't wait. I am sooooo excited!** Do you think that one day we could do one of those bush-tucker tours? I read about them in class a while ago and then looked it up on the internet. There's a company near your place that does them. I thought maybe Uncle Charlie might take us. **What do you think?** Gran, I've got to go now and do my homework (BORING!) but we'll see you really soon. Mum can't wait till we leave, I reckon. Lots of love, Sammy.

About punctuation

- Sentences end with a **full stop** (.), **question mark** (?) or **exclamation mark** (!).
- Statements end with a **full stop**; for example, **I can't wait.**
- Questions end with a **question mark**; for example, **What do you think?** Note: we don't need a question mark for a reported question; for example, *I asked Gran what she thought.* (See Chapter 14 for more on this.)
- Exclamations or words, phrases and sentences spoken loudly, excitedly or with special feeling end with an **exclamation mark**; for example, **Wow!/I am sooooo excited!/What a cool grandma you are!**
- Remember: it's best not to use too many exclamation marks in your writing—they can **lose their effect**. In most cases full stops or commas can be used; for example, **Wow! I can't believe it.** is better than *Wow! I can't believe it!*

Boost your punctuation skills

1 Add the correct end **punctuation** (? or ! or .)

For example: Why do people around the world honour Nelson Mandela?

a What hunting weapons were used by Indigenous Australians in the past____

b I wonder how people learned to find water under the desert____

c Get out____ There's a crocodile right behind you____

d The area around Lake Mungo is all Barkindji country____

e Would I catch snakes____ Not on your life____ If I leave them be, they'll leave me be too.

2 Write the missing **punctuation** in the spaces.

Teacher: Who knows how places get their names____

Lionel: My Dad says that some places have Aboriginal names that tell what happened there or what it looked like____

Teacher: That's right, Lionel. Parramatta actually means a place where eels lie down.

Matt: (beating his desk top with his fist) We are the Eels____ We are the Eels____

Teacher: Yes, we all know how you love your football team, Matt____

Alisha: I read somewhere that Katoomba means a place of falling water.

Denton: An old man told me that Gerringong, where we go for holidays, means a place of peril____

Teacher: Goodness me____ I won't be holidaying there if that's the case.

3 The end **punctuation** is wrong here. Write it correctly in the space provided.

- **a** I wonder why wild creatures appear so often in Aboriginal art? ____
- **b** What a wild experience? ____
- **c** Have you ever tried dot painting! ____
- **d** The loss of so many Aboriginal languages is a tragedy! ____
- **e** Mehmet asked Harry to tell him the story of The Rainbow Serpent? ____

4 Add a **full stop** or **question mark** to the end of these sentences.

- **a** What are the colours of the Aboriginal flag of Australia ____
- **b** Do Torres Strait Islanders have their own Australian flag ____
- **c** He asked himself if he could survive alone in the bush ____
- **d** Who was the brave Aboriginal companion who saved the explorer Kennedy ____
- **e** Mandy asked who had first lived in area where she now lived ____

5 This report lacks five end **punctuation** marks. Put them where they belong.

> How do you think you would fare in the Wild Dog Range for three whole days Two thirteen-year-olds from Smithtown recently had the chance to find this out. Searchers had almost given up hope of finding them when they heard the cry: Smoke I can see smoke.
>
> Within ten minutes James Henderson and Peter Vella had been winched to safety by helicopter. Reporters met them at the airport One asked how they came to be found so far from their planned route
>
> When the boys told of losing their compass and taking a wrong turn up a gully, they were asked how they lost it. The boys confessed that a possum had run up a tree with it and that neither of them was any good at climbing trees. An unheroic end to a great survival tale. Well done, boys

6 Using all the **punctuation** you have learned so far, punctuate these sentences correctly.

- **a** jim jackson a year 8 student mounted a display of aboriginal books and music cds
- **b** what a throw the boomerang flew twenty metres and even disappeared over the hills for a second it then curved back and flew directly into the hands of the thrower
- **c** in 2008 the Australian prime minister formally apologised to indigenous people for past wrongs.

UNIT SIX

Our region

Focus

Conjunctions; commas (4)

Grammar in use

I'd like to know more about Asia as three of my friends, Tan, Trung **and** Geraldine have Asian backgrounds. Tan came from Malaysia with his parents **when** he was little. Trung's grandparents, the Nguyens, live down the street **and** around the corner from us. We visit them **whenever** we feel hungry **because** Mrs Nguyen makes sweets to die for.

Although Geraldine has a Chinese surname her family, like mine, has been Australian for five generations. She is the cleverest **and** most generous girl in the class. She helps us boys with Maths **before** we have even asked her.

About grammar

Conjunctions

- are **joining words**. Common conjunctions are *as, and, but, or, nor, so, yet, because, when, unless, although, if, whenever, while* and *since*.
- **explain relationships** like why, when and where something happens or the order in which it happens; for example, **when** *he was little*/**whenever** *we feel hungry*/**because** *Mrs Nguyen makes sweets to die for.*
- **Conjunctions** join
  - » **words of the same kind**—nouns with nouns, verbs with verbs, pronouns with pronouns, adjectives with adjectives, and adverbs with adverbs; for example, *Tan, Trung* **and** *Geraldine*/*the cleverest* **and** *most generous.*
  - » **phrases** to other phrases; for example, *down the street* **and** *around the corner.*
  - » **clauses**—one part of a sentence to another part of a sentence; for example, *Tan came from Malaysia with his parents* **when** *he was little.*/*She helps us boys with Maths* **before** *we have even asked her.* (We will look at clauses in Chapters 11 and 12.)
- Note: conjunctions can come at the **start** of a sentence; for example, **Although** *Geraldine has a Chinese surname her family, like mine, has been Australian for five generations.*
- Some conjunctions come in **pairs**; for example, *not only … but also, neither … nor.*

Boost your grammar skills

1 Circle the **conjunction(s)** in these sentences.

a Lychees and rambutan are Asian fruits.

b Rubber trees have a brown trunk but the wood inside is white.

c Kuala Lumpur is Malaysia's capital and Jakarta is Indonesia's capital.

d In Cambodia he will visit the Angkor Wat temple if he can.

e I like writing to Rani because she tells me such interesting stories about her village.

f Whenever I pass a travel agency, I always pick up a travel brochure.

g When Mr Jones worked in Indonesia, he grew to love Java's puppet theatre.

2 Join these with the most appropriate **conjunction** from the list

and	or	nor	but

a dark ________________ beautiful jungle

b quick ________________ agile monkeys

c tired ________________ happy trekkers

d a shallow ________________ wide river

e black ________________ moonless night

f not only dark ________________ also foggy

g neither one ________________ the other

h either black ________________ white

3 Circle the correct **conjunction**.

a Thousands of tourists visit Beijing (but/and) very few have visited Wuhan.

b Dragon boat racing is very exciting (if/although) it can be quite dangerous.

c Monsoon winds bring rain to Asia (if/and) they also bring typhoons.

d Some birds migrate from Siberia to Australia (when/and) then fly back again annually.

e (Because/although) trucks are sometimes used, timber is generally moved by elephants in Thailand.

f The Mekong flows through all of Indochina since/until it reaches the South China Sea.

4 Write an appropriate **conjunction** in the space.

For example: We travelled by river ___because___ the road was cut by a landslide.

a We watched dragon boat races in Thailand ________________ we visited that country.

b You must always drink boiled water ________________ you want to avoid a stomach upset.

c We visited the flower market ________________ bought our mother some orchids.

d Sam ordered satay prawns ________________ Kellie ordered fried rice as she did not like prawns.

e The crocodile looked placid ________________ it had a nasty gleam in its eye.

f ________________ she is still learning to play it, Jessica treasures her Japanese flute.

5 Circle all the **conjunctions** in this text.

> When we set out on our trek into the jungle we were excited but we had no idea what the day would bring. Our elephant swayed constantly from side to side so we all felt sick. Although we had covered ourselves with Aerogard, we were eaten alive by mozzies. A monkey stole my hat, and then he snatched Ingrid's biscuits and ran up a tree with them. When we stopped to look at a waterfall, a spider fell onto Ingrid's shoulder. This made her scream so the elephant trumpeted loudly in fright.

6 Choose **conjunctions** from the list below to join each sentence pair. Use each only once. Some might go at the start of one of the sentences in the pair.

because	while	so	if	but	unless

a **i** China's biggest river is the Yangtze ________________

ii It has several other great rivers too.

b **i** I won't go to the crocodile display. ________________

ii I am frightened of crocodiles.

c **i** It does not rain. ________________

ii We will go to the night markets.

d **i** You aren't able to come with me. ________________

ii I won't go to the night markets this evening.

e **i** Don't go out in the sun. ________________

ii You wear a very large hat.

f **i** We visited the temple. ________________

ii Dad went on a long bush trek.

7 Join the three sentences in each set below using **conjunctions**, and take out or change any words as needed. There is more than one way to do this.

a Asian pythons are as thick as your arm and very long. They are not venomous. They only hunt small creatures.

____

____

____

____

b The last days of the dry season are terribly hot. It rains. Suddenly the air is cool and fresh.

____

____

____

____

c The sun's rays come down vertically at the Equator. It is always hot there. There is no summer or winter.

____

____

____

____

____

8 How many **conjunctions** can you find in these sentences? Write them on the lines.

a The small boy tied a flag to a long stick so his ducks would follow the flag as he took them out to graze. ______________________

b Japanese fishermen raise a lantern on a pole when they fish at night so they can attract fish. ______________________

c Because monsoon rains are very heavy, sometimes there are floods in low lying areas and people have to be evacuated. ______________________

d Although they are tiny, swallows migrate between China and Australia so they can live in continuous summer. ______________________

e Unless pandas eat mountains of bamboo shoots they will not survive because, unlike other bears, they are herbivores. ______________________

9 Write an appropriate **conjunction** in each space.

a Climbers love Guilin in China ______________ it has steep rocky mountains.

b ______________ typhoons are dangerous, they bring good rain.

c Ships must find safe harbour ______________ a typhoon is forecast.

d Do not drink unboiled water ______________ you want to get sick.

e You will make friends ______________ you learn some of the local language.

10 Brett has used four incorrect **conjunctions** in his letter. Write the sentences containing the incorrect conjunctions correctly on the lines below.

> Hey Charlie,
>
> Wish you were here. The sea is so blue because I can see the yellow sand on the sea floor. Bali's beaches are great. They are all white sand whenever you look and there are all kinds of shells on them. You can surf although snorkel. You can even ride little motorbikes on the beach because no-one is there. See you soon,
>
> Brett.

____

____

____

____

____

____

Punctuation in use

Diwali, celebrating the victory of Good over Evil, is one of India's most well-loved festivals. In English it is called the Festival of Lights because, over the five days of the festival, little oil lamps are burned day and night, in doorways and windows and along the roadside. **These lights, along with garlands of bright yellow marigolds, are symbols of the light of goodness in our lives. Diwali is mostly celebrated by Indians in India, but it is also celebrated by 30 million Indians living in other countries around the world.**

About punctuation

We use **commas**

- to help us make our **meaning clear**. They are especially useful when the sentence is long.
- to **separate long chunks of extra information** from the rest of the sentence; for example, **Diwali, celebrating the victory of Good over Evil, is one of India's most well-loved festivals. These lights, along with garlands of bright yellow marigolds, are symbols of the light of goodness in our lives.**
- to **separate two or more long statements** joined by conjunctions such as *and*, *but*, *or* and *so*; for example, **Diwali is mostly celebrated by Indians in India, but it is also celebrated by 30 million Indians living in other countries around the world**. (Note: this is a compound sentence. We will look more at these in Chapter 11.)
- wherever one is needed to **avoid confusion and misunderstanding**. Look at these sentences: *A short time after the rain began to fall./A short time after, the rain began to fall.* When reading the first sentence we are confused for a moment about the meaning. The second sentence is quite clear—the comma makes the difference.
- Note: the best guide to usage in long sentences like this is your own judgement. It helps to read the sentence **out loud** (or under your breath) and see where you need to pause. This is usually the place where you need a comma.

Boost your punctuation skills

1 Put **commas** in these sentences to mark off the long chunks of extra information. Remember to put a comma both before and after the extra words.

a Singapore an island and a city in one is the most modern city in southern Asia.

b Fiji and northern Fiji in particular has spectacular rainforests that can be explored with the help of a guide.

c The Indian cobra one of the world's most venomous snakes can inflate a threatening hood on its head.

d The zookeeper and his assistant hot in pursuit of the escaped monkeys cried out for help.

e A newcomer to Shanghai the Pearl of the Orient could be excused for being overwhelmed by its 24/7 way of life.

f The Hibiscus Festival a week-long event popular with Fiji locals and tourists alike takes place in the first week of August with parades, music and fireworks.

2 Put the missing **commas** where needed in these long compound sentences.

- **a** The Diwali Festival marks the beginning of the Hindu New Year and so many Indian businesses start a new accounting year on the Diwali Festival date.
- **b** The main language spoken in Fiji is English but most locals speak the Fijian language or Hindustani as well.
- **c** Ramadan is the ninth month of the Muslim calendar year and during this time Muslim people do not eat or drink during daylight.
- **d** Last year our school had a small multicultural day but this year we are joining with two other schools to have a combined multicultural festival.

3 Tick (✔) the sentence with the clearest meaning.

- **a i** Walking in Japanese mountains is dangerous with bears still at large in the forests there.
  - **ii** Walking in Japanese mountains is dangerous, with bears still at large in the forests there.
- **b i** The reporter interviewed a backpacker, two sisters, Freddie and Sam Wilson, and a tour guide in Phu Ket.
  - **ii** The reporter interviewed a backpacker, two sisters Freddie and Sam Wilson and a tour guide in Phu Ket.
- **c i** Crossing the Taklamakan Desert in daylight is madness with black stones reflecting fierce heat back from the ground.
  - **ii** Crossing the Taklamakan Desert in daylight is madness, with black stones reflecting fierce heat back from the ground.

4 Put **commas** in these sentences to make the meaning completely clear and correct.

- **a** During the summer days become longer and longer.
- **b** For Jenny Thomas would always be a champion.
- **c** Soon after the concert began.

5 Tick (✔) the sentences that have their **commas** correctly placed. Cross (✘) the others. Remember: reading the sentences out loud may help you.

- **a** Lee Na flew her dragon-shaped kite so high it caught in the top of a tree and hung there, its dragon tail waving forlornly in the breeze. ______
- **b** Chinese lanterns the bright red ones with silken tassels are always festive. ______
- **c** Japanese fishermen band the necks of cormorants so they can't swallow their catch, and then send them over the side of the boat to go fishing for them. ______
- **d** Water buffalo, a common sight throughout Southeast Asia, plough fields, pull carts and even, carry children to school. ______

6 Remembering all the rules about **commas** learned so far, punctuate this text correctly.

> Indonesia that volcanic chain of islands stretching from Northern Sumatra to West Irian's border with Papua New Guinea is home to people of many different ethnic groups. These include the Minangkabu of Sumatra the Javanese the Balinese the Madurese and the Dayaks of Sabah. Although in the past they all spoke different languages everyone now speaks the national language Bahasa Indonesia and so communication across the islands is easier.

UNIT SEVEN

Wrecks and other calamities

Focus

Verbs and tense; quotation marks

Grammar in use

Paul **leafed** through a diving magazine. He **dreamed** of being a professional diver and exploring the ocean's depths. He **imagined** the excitement of sweeping away the sand on the ocean floor to reveal the old iron anchor of a lost galleon. Paul lay back in the sun and pictured life aboard the ancient ship.

Men **are** everywhere. They **are scrubbing** decks, they **are climbing** rigging and they are tying down cargo. Of course, his ship **will be** one of those galleons full of gold for which the Spaniards bartered western cloth and trinkets. And, of course, he **will get** his treasure to the surface easily and be rich and famous.

About grammar

We call verb time (when things happen) **tense**.

There are three basic tenses: **present**, **past** and **future**.

- **Present tense** shows what is happening now; for example, *Men* **are** *everywhere.*
- **Past tense** tells us about events in the past; for example, Paul **leafed** *through a diving magazine./He* **dreamed** *of being.*
- **Future tense** tells us about the future; for example, *his ship* **will be** *one of those galleons/he* **will get** *his treasure.*
- We show **continuous action** with auxiliary verbs and the *ing* form of the verb; for example, **are scrubbing**, **are climbing**. We can show continuous action in all tenses (*are scrubbing, were scrubbing, will be scrubbing*).
- There are three **past-tense forms**. Look at these different sentences and think about the different uses of the tenses. (The names of these tenses are in brackets but you don't need to know these names.)
  - » *He* **imagined** *life as a diver.* (This is called the simple past.)
  - » *He* **has imagined** *life as a diver for three years.* (This is called the present perfect.)
  - » *He* **had imagined** *life as a diver but now realised it was not to be.* (This is called the past perfect.)
- Most **past tense** forms follow a regular pattern formed with *ed*, but some are irregular. For example:

  see → saw → has seen | *draw → drew → has drawn*
  break → broke → has broken | *do → did → has done*
- Generally all main verbs in a text are written in the same tense. However, if things happen at different times (as in the text above) we need to **change the verb tenses** to show this.

Boost your grammar skills

1 Write the **tense** of each sentence (present, past or future).

For example: The old Swedish warship, Vasa, sank just outside Stockholm Harbour. past

a Many people today enjoy wreck diving for recreation. ____________

b The *Titanic* sank to the ocean floor. ____________

c No-one will raise the *Titanic* because it will break up in the process. ____________

d Most treasure hunters hope to find a sunken Spanish galleon full of Inca gold. ____________

e Pirates have sailed the open seas for many centuries. ____________

2 Rewrite these in the **tense** named.

For example: Typhoons sank any small vessel in Asian waters. (future)
Typhoons will sink any small ship in Asian waters.

a The whale surfaces and spouts water from its vent. (past)

____

b Divers always wore pressure suits when they were diving. (present)

____

c In polar regions ships' crews will fear iceberg contact. (present)

____

d Badly loaded cargo will sink a small ship. (past)

____

e Great tankers load tonnes of oil at terminals in the Middle East. (future)

____

3 Circle the **verb** that is in the correct **tense**.

a The *Exxon Valdez* once (caused/causes) a huge oil slick along the Alaskan coast.

b The *Mary Celeste* was found adrift but no crew or passengers (are/were) aboard.

c When a ship sinks it most often (went/goes) down bow first.

d When the *Mary Rose* was salvaged her cannon balls (explodes/exploded) on contact with the air.

4 Write the underlined **verbs** in the appropriate continuous form. Keep the same **tense** (i.e. present or past).

For example: Firemen fought a blaze in a high rise building. were fighting

a Sailors battled towering waves and wild winds. ____________

b The green tugboats haul grain ships into the bay. ____________

c Fishermen dragged in nets of silver fish. ____________

d Cranes lift containers from the decks of cargo carriers. ____________

e Lone sailors take great risks on the open seas. ____________

5 Correct the **tense** of the **verbs** so that they follow the tense of the first sentence.

Bushfires are part of every Australian's experience. They were ________________ not confined just to the bush. Heat, wind and lack of rain raised ________________ the risk of fire to Extreme in any location, especially when there was ________________ plenty of dry grass around. It took ________________ only seconds for a fire to take hold when these conditions are present. A cigarette butt, a spark from a barbecue or a flash of lightning started ________________ a fire in a flash.

6 Rewrite these in the present **tense**.

a The wind howled and there was no moon.

____

b Lighthouse signals were visible in the dark.

____

c The freighter's engines failed under the weight of the stormy sea.

____

d At a frightening speed the ship surged towards the cliff and broke up.

____

e Many sailors have dreamed of circumnavigating the globe alone.

____

7 The underlined **verbs** are in the wrong tense. What **tense** should they be? Write present, past or future.

a In 1629 the Dutch ship *Batavia* will crash on the barren West Australian coast. ________________

b If sailors ignore typhoon alerts they risked being sunk. ________________

c The location of the lost *HMAS Sydney* in 2010 will be a wonderful discovery. ________________

d If you go to the Naval Museum I went with you. ________________

e The story of the *Titanic* is captivating the world since 1912. ________________

f A lighthouse steers sailors to port and warned them of danger. ________________

8 Rewrite the following in the future **tense**.

I must write an essay on the wreck of the *Batavia*. I have a book from the library about the wreck so I can get the facts straight before I write.

____

____

____

____

Punctuation in use

Talent Night—August 16, 7 pm

Norwood High School is staging another Talent Night. You might think this very brave after last year's disaster with the wild storms and eventual blackout, but the show must go on, as they say. Highlights will include a scene from Shakespeare's **'Romeo and Juliet'**, a Year 9 presentation of a song medley from **'Grease'** and a Year 8 all-male rap item called 'Waiting in the Tuckshop Queue'. **Ben 'Wilko' Wilkins** will demonstrate disco dancing backed by the Year 7 band. After Interval there's an open mike session when anyone can take the stage for his or her **'two minutes of fame'** regardless of whether they are pitch perfect or tone deaf.

About punctuation

- **Quotation marks** can be single ('a') or double ("a") for reported speech but they must be the same all through the text. These days, single quotation marks are more common. In typed text we use *italics* instead of quotation marks for titles of books and films; for example, *Romeo and Juliet*. However, we use single quotation marks for the titles of poems, songs, short stories and articles.
- Quotation marks or italics are used to show
  - » the **titles** of books, films, CDs, songs, etc. in a sentence; for example, Shakespeare's **'Romeo and Juliet'**/medley from **'Grease'**.
  - » a **nickname** after someone's real name; for example, *Ben* **'Wilko'** *Wilkins*.
  - » an **unusual or particular usage** of a word; for example, **'two minutes of fame'** (sarcastic), a **'method'** actor (specialist term).
- Note: we enclose small words at the start of titles (*A*, *An*, *The*) if they are **part of those titles**; for example, *'A Tale of Two Cities'*, *'The Age'*, not *A 'Tale of Two Cities'*, *The 'Age'*.

Boost your punctuation skills

1 Put in **quotation marks** where necessary.

- **a** Gulliver's Travels was written by Jonathan Swift.
- **b** Jurassic Park was originally a book by Michael Crichton.
- **c** The songs from the musical, Cats, have been recorded by many singers.
- **d** Australia's national anthem is Advance Australia Fair.
- **e** Sesame Street, the children's TV show, has been around for nearly fifty years.

2 Put in the **quotation marks** Craig has forgotten in this school bulletin entry.

Our library has just acquired a large batch of new books and magazines. There are the latest Street Cars and All Terrain Vehicles magazines for the auto enthusiasts as well as a CD in the back of Street Cars for all the great street car sound effects. There's even a great new Kawasaki manual with cross-section diagrams called Off-Road Racing.

3 Tick (✔) the correctly punctuated sentences and cross (✘) the wrong ones.

a Martha and Rebecca hired 'the DVD Happy Feet'. ______

b For her birthday Claudia asked for the book 'Lionheart' by Jesse Martin. ______

c David Attenborough's 'wildlife films' are fascinating. ______

d Mitchell 'Titch' Johnson is a member of the Rural Fire Service. ______

e Little Zac choked his way through grandma's 'delicious' spinach and sprout pie. ______

4 Add any missing punctuation to this recount of a lunchtime drama rehearsal. Check for missing or incorrect capitals, **quotation marks** and commas.

> Mr James wanted everyone present including cast lighting people and prompts. I didn't think I wanted to see shakespeare's Play Hamlet on stage on such a hot sticky day but it was worth it to see Ben play hamlet and leap about the stage in tights. Oscar was reading Tim Winton's Blue Boy and missed it all, even the bit where Ben talked to a skull, so of course he doesn't understand why Ben's new nickname is Skull.

5 These sentences have no **punctuation marks**. Write them correctly underneath. Think carefully about the last one.

a mr swan said these were easy so how come these easy maths questions are so hard to do

____

b my mates all go by their own names except tom who prefers his nickname fitzy

____

c shelve all the A-title books over there starting with arthur the aardvark

____

d grandfather used to sing a great little song called my marvellous toy did you ever hear it

____

e some people prefer pie-in-your-face humour to clever, witty dialogue.

____

6 Fix any errors in these sentences. Some **quotation marks** are correctly used, some are not and some are missing.

a David is listening to rap music and watching The Hunger Games at the same time.

b That documentary's 'soundtrack' sounds like one called 'The Flight of the Condor'.

c It's only a 'fine' day if you're a penguin; it's 'cold and wet' out there.

d Have you read the 'Count of Monte Cristo'? I haven't, but I have seen the 'DVD'.

e Every age has its 'in' word a word everyone uses for six months, then forgets again.

7 The following is **correctly punctuated**. True or false?

Marley ate 'Smiths Crisps' while watching the musical 'Cats' and distressed other viewers.

____

____

UNIT EIGHT

Out in space

Focus

Subjects and subject–verb agreement; abbreviations

Grammar in use

The Hubble space telescope **is expanding** our knowledge of the universe, but what no-one expected was the sheer beauty of the wonders it is revealing. **Great cloud pillars** of dust and **rainbow-coloured** gases appear in the Hubble images. **Newborn** stars spit fire and gas into the roiling cloud even as we watch.

Our planet Earth **seems** ancient. However, **it** is a mere infant compared to the age of the universe. Yet the universe now is only in its second stage of development, the Stelliferous or Starry Age. We **recognise** very local star clusters or constellations by name. One such **constellation**, the Southern Cross, **lights** our night sky.

About grammar

- As you saw in Chapter 4, the **subject** of a sentence is who or what the sentence is about (usually a noun). The **predicate** is the rest of the sentence which tells us about the subject. The predicate includes the verb; for example, *Our planet Earth* (subject) **seems** *ancient* (predicate). *We* (subject) **recognise** *very local star clusters or constellations by name* (predicate).
- We identify the subject of a sentence by asking **who** or **what** before the verb; for example, Who or what **seems** *ancient*? *Our planet Earth* is the answer and therefore the subject.
- Subjects are usually, but not always, the **first word** in a sentence; for example, *However,* **it** *is a mere infant compared to the age of universe.* Here, *it* is the subject.
- A subject may include adjectives or other words around the noun to form **a noun group**; for example, **Newborn** *stars*/**Great cloud pillars** *of dust and* **rainbow-coloured** *gases.*
- **Verbs** must **agree in number** with their subject—either singular or plural; for example, *The Hubble space telescope* **is expanding** *our knowledge* (not *telescope are expanding*)/*Our planet Earth* **seems** *ancient* (not *Our planet Earth seem ancient*).
- **Collective nouns are usually singular** and are followed by a singular verb; for example, *One such* **constellation** (collective noun), *the Southern Cross,* **lights** (singular verb) *our night sky.*
- Words like *one, everyone, someone, anyone, nobody* (types of pronouns) or nouns with *any, each* or *every* before them are **singular**; for example, **Each** *star* **is** *billions of years old.*
- When a sentence begins with *there* or *here,* the verb number depends on the number of the **following nouns**; for example, *There* **is** *a rocket* but *There* **are** *many stars.*

Boost your grammar skills

1 Underline the **subject** in each sentence. Remember: it may be more than one word, and it may not be the first word in the sentence.

- **a** Our sun emits immensely hot solar flares.
- **b** The white-tiled space shuttle made many trips into space and back.
- **c** The first lunar landing team were Neil Armstrong, Michael Collins and "Buzz" Aldrin.
- **d** Tragically, in the Apollo 7 disaster the whole space crew was killed.
- **e** In 2012, China launched its first manned space mission.

2 Write the **verb** that matches the **subject** in number.

- **a** The earth ______________ around the sun. (revolve/revolves)
- **b** Six gaseous rings ______________ the planet Saturn. (circle/circles)
- **c** No-one now ______________ the moon is made of cheese. (believes/believe)
- **d** There ______________ four gaseous planets in our solar system. (is/are)
- **e** Water ______________ not appear to exist on Mars. (does/do)
- **f** Each astronaut ______________ years of space experience. (have/has)

3 Circle the helping **verb** which agrees in number with the sentence **subject**.

- **a** Satellites (have/has been) put in space for all sorts of purposes.
- **b** Satellite navigation (was/were) first invented for ships.
- **c** The Hubble telescope (is/are still) transmitting images to earth.
- **d** In the past meteors (have/has) struck the earth with calamitous results.
- **e** Jupiter's four main moons (is/are) called Io, Europa, Ganymede and Callisto.

4 Write the correct form of the **verb** (singular or plural) in the spaces.

- **a** The crew of the space station (rotate) ______________ every six months.
- **b** The star cluster called The Pleiades (shine) ______________ in the Southern Hemisphere.
- **c** Space junk (burn) ______________ up on re-entry to the earth's atmosphere.
- **d** Not all stars (twinkle) ______________ as brightly as others.
- **e** A meteor shower, when it happens, (be) ______________ a spectacular show.

5 Cross (✗) the sentences with incorrect **verbs**.

- **a** An asteroid's impact crater on Earth are called a Cenote Ring. __________
- **b** Pluto's moon, Charon, is named after the mythological ferryman who rows people over the river Styx to Hades. __________
- **c** Halley's, Hale-Bopp and Shoemaker Levy 9 is the names of well-known comets. __________
- **d** Among the planets, Mars is known as the red planet. __________

6 Connect these **subjects** and **predicates** with a line so that all five sentences make sense.

a The Southern Cross, with its five stars,	lasts only eighty-eight days.
b The zodiac signs of Aries, Taurus and Gemini	are from one to three eclipses.
c A small cloud, called Scooter for its speed,	are also constellations in space.
d Mercury's year	circles the planet Neptune.
e In some years there	is unique to the Southern Hemisphere.

7 Edit Max's report for any errors (**tense** or **subject–verb agreement**). Cross out the errors and write the correct **verbs** below them.

> Comets blazes a trail of fire across the night sky. Some comets has a long life so they reappear regularly. Halley's Comet came around every seventy-six years and will next be seen in 2061. The Hale-Bopp comet were last seen in 1995 and will not been around for another 2365 years. At present astronomers will list almost 1000 comets, but there are several thousand in our solar system which remains unseen.

8 Circle the correct **verb** in each pair so these space travel directions make sense.

> We (is/are) departing from Galactic Base One at the South Celestial Pole for Dorado, via the constellation of Hydra, and then we (travel/travels) on to Phoenix. On Phoenix we (collect/collects) the reports of Sky Master Jackson. We (knows/know) they (are/is) stored in the base vault. Security Officer Wilbow (have/has) vault access so he will give them to us instead of Jackson, who now (run/runs) Black Hole Surveillance Operations. To return home the recommendation is that we (proceeds/proceed) directly to Galactic Intelligence headquarters. They (think/thinks) the reports (is/are) invaluable for future intelligence planning.

9 Circle the correct **verb** in each pair. Consider **tense** as well as **subject–verb agreement**.

> The possibility of life on other planets (is/are) always a serious consideration. If people do not live on a planet, what else (did/does)? It is possible that some organisms (breathe/breathed) something other than oxygen and that others might (survive/survives) the freezing temperatures we cannot. Scientists (is/are) currently looking at the possibility of bacterial life on other planets.

Punctuation in use

Larry is always on the lookout for funny names like Sly, Sly and Bent **Pty Ltd**, Solicitors and Drs Kneebone and Knuckley, Orthopaedic Surgeons. Other funny ones in his collection are Bliss and **Co.** Sweets Factory and JK Dead (Funeral Director). Larry loves acronyms too. Even though most acronyms are serious like **NASA** (National Aeronautics and Space Administration), he knows lots of funny ones too. However, I suspect he might have made some of them up, like his favourite, DAFT which he claims stands for Dust and Aerosol Fug Test. **Dr** Andrew Pike of Mt Stromlo Observatory had never heard of it when we visited there.

About punctuation

- An **abbreviation is a shortened form** of a word or words. Abbreviations can be made from:
  - the **first letters of the original words**; for example, *ABC* for *Australian Broadcasting Corporation*
  - the **first few letters**; for example, *Tas. for Tasmania*
  - from **selected letters**; for example, *Pty Ltd (Proprietary Limited), Co. (Company)*. (If the original words have capitals, so too do the abbreviations.)
- An **acronym** is a word made up of the first letters of the main words without any full stops; for example, **NASA**, originally from *National Aeronautics and Space Administration*, and **RADAR**, meaning *radio detecting and ranging*, are now used as single words.
- An **abbreviation is followed by a full stop** if the last letter is not the last letter of the original word; for example, *Capt. Stevens (Captain), Tas. (Tasmania), Thurs. (Thursday).*
- An **abbreviation has no full stop** if the last letter of the original and of the abbreviation are the same; for example, **Dr** *(Doctor)*, **Mt** *(Mount)*, **Bros** *(Brothers)*.
- **Abbreviations** are sometimes used to **shorten common phrases**, but often the original words are Latin. So the abbreviation of *for example* is *e.g.*, which stands for *exempli gratia*. Other such abbreviations are *i.e.* (*id est* = *that is*), *etc.* (*et cetera* = *and so on*), *am* (*ante meridian* = *before noon*) and *pm* (*post meridian* = *after noon*).
- **Abbreviations are being invented all the time**. *ASAP*, for example, is now commonly used for *as soon as possible*. Of course, text messaging is bringing many abbreviations into our language; for example, *LOL* for *laugh out loud*, *AAK* for *asleep at keyboard* and *BFF* for *best friends forever*.
- In general we **use abbreviations more often in informal writing**.

Boost your punctuation skills

1 Write the commonly used **abbreviations** for the following.

a Royal Australian Air Force ____________

b Commonwealth Scientific and Industrial Research Organisation ____________

c Member of Parliament ____________

d personal computer ____________

e four-wheel drive ____________

f Eastern Standard Time ____________

2 Write the commonly used **acronyms** for these.

a Australian Security and Intelligence Organisation ____________

b Queensland and Northern Territory Airlines ____________

c North Atlantic Treaty Organisation ____________

d Light Amplification by Stimulated Emission of Radiation ____________

e Australian and New Zealand Army Corps ____________

f self-contained underwater breathing apparatus ____________

3 Write **acronyms** for these imaginary groups.

a Legal Association of Wandering Stars ____________

b Galactic Assembly of Sparkling Stars ____________

c Fifth Intergalactic Games Series ____________

d Martian Arms Manufacturing Association ____________

4 **Abbreviate** the following place names as they would appear on a map.

a Mount Kosciusko ____________

b Fairy Hole Road ____________

c Victoria ____________

d Smith Street ____________

e Whitlam Crescent ____________

f Murrumbidgee Avenue ____________

5 What do these **abbreviations** mean?

a co. ____________

b Sgt ____________

c jnr ____________

d DVD ____________

e dept ____________

f est. ____________

g pt ____________

h SMS ____________

6 Write **abbreviations** for January, February, April, August, September, October, November and December.

____

____

____

____

7 Tick (✔) the sentences correctly punctuated and put a cross (✘) next to those incorrectly punctuated.

a Capt. James Kirk of the *SS Enterprise* had the help of Mr Spock. ______

b Payment must be made by Mon 13, 2016. ______

c Mrs. Southwell reads a lot of science fiction. ______

d Hall Bros. supply fine copper wire for space use. ______

e Start and Stop Traffic Management Pty Ltd has gone bankrupt. ______

8 Write down five text messaging **abbreviations** you know of—the abbreviated forms and the full forms.

____

____

____

____

____

____

____

____

____

____

____

9 Circle the correct **acronyms** and **abbreviations** in this newspaper report.

Two girls missing from Red Rock School were found late yesterday at the base of (Mt./Mt) Misery. They had been part of a school Fun Run and lost their way, taking Henley (Blvd/Boulvd) instead of Long Point (Dr./Dr).

The younger of the two had broken her ankle and was airlifted by (medivac/Medivac) to Yellow Plains Hospital for treatment.

The elder girl regretted not having her (i-phone/iPhone) with her. She would have texted (sos/SOS) and directions to save everyone a lot of trouble. And maybe I need a new pair of Nikes from Patrick (Bros/Broths.) in town

Revision Test 2

Grammar

Shade one circle to show the correct answer.

1 Which line contains only prepositions?

- ◯ and, car, are, is, here, over
- ◯ was, will, can, as, under, drive
- ◯ near, on, after, in, beside, to
- ◯ even, no, were, up, though, into

2 Which circled word is the preposition?

(Rings) of coloured (gas) (around) Saturn make (it) a beautiful planet.

- ◯ Rings
- ◯ around
- ◯ gas
- ◯ it

3 Which underlined word group is the prepositional phrase?

The (evening star) rises (in the east).

- ◯ evening star
- ◯ in the east

4 Which underlined group of words is a prepositional phrase?

- ◯ Walking on the moon was once <u>sheer imagination</u>.
- ◯ Walking on the moon was <u>once sheer imagination</u>.
- ◯ Walking <u>on the moon</u> was once sheer imagination.
- ◯ <u>Walking</u> on the moon was once sheer imagination.

5 Which line contains only conjunctions?

- ◯ desert, river, because, through, after
- ◯ market, fruit, but, until, cheap
- ◯ when, so, and, unless, because
- ◯ over, below, as, does, although

6 Which conjunction correctly joins these two words?

cold ______________ wet

- ◯ and
- ◯ but
- ◯ because
- ◯ then
- ◯ so

7 Which conjunction correctly joins these word groups?

still sleepy ______________ ready to go

- ◯ because
- ◯ and
- ◯ although
- ◯ as
- ◯ but

8 Which conjunction correctly joins these sentences?

Astronauts are weightless. They are in space.

- ◯ unless
- ◯ until
- ◯ because
- ◯ when
- ◯ then

9 Which sentence is correct?

- ◯ Volcanoes in Java is erupting right now.
- ◯ Volcanoes in Java was erupting right now.
- ◯ Volcanoes in Java are erupting right now.

10 Which verb completes this sentence correctly?

Charlie Wilkinson ______________ at the Leeton Eisteddfod later this year.

- ◯ sings
- ◯ did sing
- ◯ will sing
- ◯ sang

In questions 11–12, which helping verb completes the sentence correctly?

11 Timber cutting ______________ threatening the habitat of many animals in Kalimantan today.

- ◯ was
- ◯ are
- ◯ is
- ◯ has

12 James ______________ seen all the Star Wars films.

- ◯ have
- ◯ has
- ◯ was
- ◯ can

13 Which of the following correctly completes the sentence?

The Khoury family ______________ in Fiji until August last year.

- ◯ is living
- ◯ will live
- ◯ lived
- ◯ are living

14 Which sentence is correct?

- ◯ Kai went swimming yesterday and will swim again next Friday.
- ◯ Kai went swimming yesterday and swam next Friday.

15 Which verb correctly completes the sentence?

Tomorrow ______________ cold and overcast.

- ◯ was
- ◯ is
- ◯ will be
- ◯ were

16 In which sentence below is the subject underlined?

- ◯ The football team in red <u>won all their matches.</u>
- ◯ <u>The football team in red</u> won all their matches.
- ◯ <u>The football team</u> in red won all their matches.
- ◯ The football team in red won <u>all their matches.</u>

17 Which sentence is correct?

- ◯ Each of the elephants are enjoying its bath in the river.
- ◯ Each of the elephants are enjoying their bath in the river.
- ◯ Each of the elephants is enjoying its bath in the river.
- ◯ Each of the elephants is enjoying their bath in the river.

Punctuation

1 Which end punctuation is missing from the sentence?

In what country is the Mt Vesuvius volcano

- ◯ ?
- ◯ !
- ◯ .
- ◯ ,

In questions 2–6, which sentence is correctly punctuated?

2
- ◯ Which planet is closer to the sun, Mercury or Venus.
- ◯ Which planet is closer to the sun, Mercury or Venus!
- ◯ Which planet is closer to the sun, Mercury or Venus?

3
- ◯ I wonder if Darwin's wet season will come early this year.
- ◯ I wonder if Darwin's wet season will come early this year?
- ◯ I wonder if Darwin's wet season will come early this year!

4
- ◯ Why is it hottest at the equator.
- ◯ Why is it hottest at the Equator?
- ◯ Why is it hottest at the Equator!

5
- ◯ no two bushfires are the same or behave the same.
- ◯ No two bushfires are the same or behave the same
- ◯ No two bushfires are the same or behave the same.

6 ◯ The trekkers wanted to get to the camp by nightfall but they had to give up their goal because of heavy rain.
◯ The trekkers wanted to get to the camp, by nightfall but they had to give up their goal because of heavy rain.
◯ The trekkers wanted, to get to the camp by nightfall, but they had to give up their goal because of heavy rain.
◯ The trekkers wanted to get to the camp by nightfall, but they had to give up their goal because of heavy rain.

7 Shade two circles to show where the missing quotation marks should go.

Ian has just finished reading ◯ a book, ◯ Gulliver's Travels, ◯ by Jonathan Swift ◯ .

In questions 8–9, shade one circle to show the words that should be in quotation marks.

8 Did you see Men in Black III at the cinema or on DVD?

Men in Black III ◯ cinema ◯ DVD ◯

9 Dorothea McKellar's description of Australia as a sunburnt country is very true.

Dorothea McKellar's description ◯ a sunburnt country ◯

In questions 10–13, which sentence has the correct punctuation?

10 ◯ 'Spinach,' of course, is every child's favourite vegetable.
◯ Spinach, of course, is every child's 'favourite' vegetable.
◯ Spinach, of course, is 'every child's' favourite vegetable.

11 ◯ 'Up There, Cazaly' has become an AFL football anthem.
◯ Up There Cazaly has become an AFL football anthem.
◯ Up There, Cazaly has become an 'AFL football anthem'.

12 ◯ Mr and Mrs. Jones lived in Japan for three years.
◯ Mr. and Mrs. Jones lived in Japan for three years.
◯ Mr. and Mrs Jones lived in Japan for three years.
◯ Mr and Mrs Jones lived in Japan for three years.

13 ◯ Who is the author of Storm Boy?
◯ Who is the author of 'Storm Boy'?
◯ Who is the author of 'Storm Boy'.
◯ Who is the 'author' of Storm Boy.

UNIT NINE

On the wings of fantasy

Focus

Adjectives; apostrophes of contraction

Grammar in use

The **old red** dragon leaned her **huge** head closer to Ping as if she wanted a **better** look. Ping could feel her **warm** breath on her face. She was a **formidable** beast. Her horns branched many times and were at least three feet long. She had a long, shaggy beard beneath her chin and the whiskers hanging on either side of her mouth were **blue**. Her eyes were **cloudy** and Ping guessed that her **dragon** sight was fading.

The old dragon made a **metallic** sound that reminded Ping of someone chinking coins together in **cupped** hands. It wasn't like any of the sounds that Kai or Danzi had made. Ping waited for the words to form in her head but none did.

(from 'Dragon Moon' by Carole Wilkinson)

About grammar

- **Adjectives describe or give information** about nouns and pronouns. They tell us about colour, shape, size, weight, age, number, quantity, sound, taste, feel and direction; for example, **old red** *dragon*/**huge** *head*/**better** *look*/**warm** *breath*/**formidable** *beast*.
- Adjectives usually come **in front of a noun** but they can also **follow the verb** *be* (e.g. *is, was*) and other verbs such as *seem, look, feel, taste, sound* and *become* (e.g. *whiskers were* **blue**/*eyes were* **cloudy**).
- Sometimes we **use a noun as an adjective** to describe something; for example, **dragon** *sight*. We can also make adjectives from parts of the verb *(ing* or *ed* verb forms); for example, **cupped** *hands*.
- Adjectives take the endings *er* and *est* to show that **two or more things are being compared**; for example, *old, older, oldest*.
- We call the *er* form of adjectives **comparative adjectives**—we use this form to compare two things. We call the *est* form **superlative adjectives**—we use this form to compare more than two things.
- Adjectives of **more than one syllable** do not add *er* and *est*. Instead we place the words *more* or *most* before them; for example, **formidable** → *more formidable* → *most formidable*, **metallic** → *more metallic* → *most metallic*.
- Note: **adjectives ending in *y*** (regardless of the number of syllables) add *er* and *est* but change the *y* to *i*; for example, **cloudy** → *cloudier* → *cloudiest*/*lovely* → *lovelier* → *loveliest*.
- A few adjectives **cannot be compared**; for example, *unique, excellent, dead, right* and *wrong*. That is, we can't say *He is more dead than she is*.

* We show **negative comparison** by using the words *less* or *least* before the adjective; for example, *less* **warm** → *least warm/less* **formidable** → *least formidable.*
* Two common adjectives **change completely** in their comparative forms. They are *good* → *better* → *best, bad* → *worse* → *worst.*

Boost your grammar skills

1 Circle the **adjectives** on the right that could be used to describe the nouns in each case.

a dog	ferocious, yapping, narrow, spiky
b cat	tabby, striped, friendly, stormy
c cow	placid, slithery, crooked, cranky
d horse	tall, shaggy, tethered, papery
e mosquito	buzzing, soft, vicious, cute
f lambs	brilliant, cuddly, bleating, straight

2 Underline any **adjective** of colour in this passage and circle any other adjectives you find.

> Snowy white unicorns, with curled and gilded horns jutting from the centre of their foreheads, played in the ghostly moonlight. Tall trees cast long black shadows over the grass where their hooves kicked up flowers and little tufts of emerald grass. The night was cool and clear and silent. Magic was in the air.

3 Underline any noun used as an **adjective** in this text. The first one has been done for you.

> His cloak was coal black, his hat was charcoal and he carried a thin black cane. He was a creature from the shadow world, this strange fellow with his claw fingers, hawk nose and gravel voice.

4 Complete these with appropriate **adjectives** from the list. The first one has been done for you.

yellow furry long flower spiralled green magic fairy lazy red tiny mythical flickering blue

a The fourth Doctor Who wore a long scarf with red, green, blue and yellow stripes.

b The man waved his ______________ wand and produced a ______________ rabbit from his hat.

c In the hot breath of the dragon were ______________ tongues of fire.

d Among the seven dwarves only one was ______________ and did not work.

e ______________ tales often include ______________ elves and fairies who play in ______________ gardens.

f A unicorn is a ______________ white horse with one ______________ horn in the middle of his forehead.

5 Circle the **adjectives** in these sentences.

a The Snow Queen lines in an ice cavern.

b A treasure chest lies buried in the sand.

c A magic carpet carried them over mountain ranges.

d The magician wears a swallow-tailed coat.

e Hairy evil-eyed trolls inhabit Scandinavian legends.

6 Complete this table about **adjectives**. The first one has been done for you.

Simple	Comparative	Superlative
strange	stranger	strangest
	odder	
		weirdest
agile		
	more skilled	
		friendliest
fearsome		

7 Complete these sentences using the superlative form of the **adjective** on the right.

a That is the ______________________ frog in the pond. (ugly)

b This is the ______________________ spell in the wizard's book of spells. (hard)

c The black dragon is the ______________________ dragon in the land. (terrible)

d Dragonflies have the ______________________ wings of all insects. (delicate)

e She was the ______________________ girl in the land. (beautiful)

8 Complete these sentences with the comparative form of the **adjective** on the right.

a James is ______________________ than Marcus. (outgoing)

b Monkeys are ______________________ than lizards. (mischievous)

c Chinese dragons are ______________________ than European dragons. (colourful)

d Leprechauns look ______________________ than elves. (odd)

e I think vampires are ______________________ than all other monsters. (scary)

9 Write the correct form of the **adjective** on the right in the gap.

a This was the ______________________ summer the Snow Queen had ever endured. (bad)

b He aimed to be the ______________________ student in the Wizard's Academy. (good)

c Medicine tastes ______________________ the longer you delay swallowing it. (bad)

d Ellen is ______________________ at making spooky noises than Esther. (good)

e Kimiko is very ______________________ at magic tricks. (good)

10 Tick (✔) the sentences which use **adjectives** correctly and cross (✘) those that are incorrect.

a The tribe came from the most distant galaxy in the universe. ____

b The challenges they faced were terribler than those faced in the last kingdom. ____

c Mara had to be the most brave she could be to rescue her friend from death. ____

d She found herself in the darkest and most terrifying part of the forest. ____

e The swirling mist seemed to become more close every time they looked back. ____

f The little boy was more calmer than his big tough-talking brothers. ____

Punctuation in use

Kai **didn't** believe in ghosts but the gloomy atmosphere frightened him. It **wasn't** that he thought spirits would come drifting through the walls. It was more that he felt unsure about what the old house held, and what might or **mightn't** suddenly happen. Even the creaking of its old timbers scared him witless. If he got back to the street in one piece, **he'd** never venture into the place again. His father's words rang in his ears: "You mustn't go into that derelict house, son."

About punctuation

- We **shorten or contract** some words for easy communication. We do this by leaving out or omitting letters. (See Chapter 16.)
- We show **contraction** by putting an **apostrophe** in the place of the missing letters; for example, *did* **n***o***t** → *did***n't**, *was* **n***o***t** → *was***n't**, *might* **n***o***t** → *might***n't**, *he* **would** → *he'***d**.
- **Common contractions** occur with **pronouns** and **auxiliary** (helping) **verbs**:
  - *is not → isn't, do not → don't, does not → doesn't, I have → I've, we are → we're, they had → they'd, there is → there's, I will → I'll, could have → could've*
    Note: *will not → won't*
- We also **make contractions** when we use a helping verb (especially *is* and *was*) after a noun; for example, *Percy's here → Percy is here, The unicorn's gone → The unicorn has gone.*
- Some **contractions sound exactly the same as other words** (These are called **homophones**.) Be careful with these ones:
  - *we're/where/wear*; for example, **We're** *(we are) going skating now.* **Where** *are my skating boots? I must* **wear** *them.*
  - *they're/there/their*; for example, **They're** *(they are) all eating* **their** *apples over* **there** *under the tree.*
  - *who's/whose*; for example, **Who's** *(who is) going to the library with me?* **Whose** *book is that?*
  - *it's/its*; for example, **It's** *(it is) quite certain the door fell off* **its** *hinges.*
  - *your/you're*; for example, **You're** *(you are) going to be late for the bus if you wait for* **your** *friend.*
- Note: take care when writing ***have* contractions**. Because they can sound like the weak pronunciation of the preposition *of*, they are often mistakenly written that way; for example, *could've* (not 'could of'), *must've* (not 'must of'), *would've* (not 'would of').

Boost your punctuation skills

1 Write the full form of the **contraction** in the gaps after the underlined words.

a He hasn't ______________ ______________ done his homework.

b She doesn't ______________ ______________ like leeks.

c They won't ______________ ______________ attend the parade.

d They haven't ______________ ______________ arrived yet.

e They've ______________ ______________ won again.

f He'd ______________ ______________ fallen.

2 Write the **contraction** of the underlined words in the spaces.

a Erin could not ______________________ see herself abseiling down that cliff face with safety.

b Mitchell would have ______________________ come but he came down with the flu.

c I have ______________________ watched my brother hang-gliding many times.

d He need not ______________________ finish the whole assignment today.

e They should have ______________________ waited for us.

f They would ______________________ soon realise their mistake.

3 Write the appropriate **contraction** in the gaps.

hasn't	I'll	he'd	I've	there's	that's

______________________ be back by five o'clock. ______________________ what he told me. ______________________ been waiting for an hour and ______________________ still no sign of him. I hope he ______________________ lost his way and ended up in the Valley of Giant Snails.

4 These **contractions** have been written without their apostrophes. Write them correctly.

a didnt ______________________

b wont ______________________

c havent ______________________

d hasnt ______________________

e hed ______________________

f shouldnt ______________________

g cant ______________________

h dont ______________________

i theyve ______________________

j mustnt ______________________

k doesnt ______________________

l werent ______________________

5 Write the **contraction** *who's* or the pronoun *whose* in the gaps as appropriate.

a ____________________ going to the magic show at lunchtime?

b ____________________ magician's wand is this?

c ____________________ going to rescue the little dragonling from the lake?

d That's the dragon ____________________ scales shine green and gold in the sun.

e ____________________ the boy in the mask?

6 Write the **contraction** *they're* or the pronoun *their* in the gaps as appropriate.

a ____________________ all trying to make the white rabbit disappear.

b ____________________ cloaks flapped and ____________________ top hats all fell off when the wind blew.

c ____________________ not looking where ____________________ going.

d All seven dragons breathed fire from ____________________ nostrils.

e It's not what ____________________ saying, it's how ____________________ saying it.

7 Write the **contraction** *it's* or the pronoun *its* in the gaps as appropriate.

a The black cat combed ____________________ whiskers thoughtfully.

b ____________________ a bird! ____________________ a plane!
No, ____________________ Superman!

c Unless ____________________ safe and comfortable ____________________ not for me.

d ____________________ the most beautiful castle in the kingdom.

e The terrible monster opened ____________________ jaw for the last time and died.

8 Circle the correct word.

a (Where/We're/Wear) are all the trapeze artists?

b (We're/Where/Wear) off to see the wizard, the wonderful wizard of Oz.

c (Where/We're/Wear) have all the frogs disappeared?

d (Where/We're/Wear) is my uniform. I need to (where/we're/wear) it today.

e (Where/We're/Wear) three blind mice. Three blind mice are we! (Where/We're/Wear) all going to a cheesy feast, (we're/where/wear) no cat beast will be!

9 Circle any **apostrophe** errors or misspellings. Write the corrections in the spaces.

a A black cat in your path is'nt bad luck. ____________________

b Casting a spell's just saying words that hav'ent any meaning. ____________________

c Ghosts and goblins aren't real, theyr'e imaginary. ____________________

d Pinocchio's nose was'nt always long. ____________________

e They dident know which path to take. ____________________

f That troll doesn't like hiding under bridges. ____________________

g Ooh, a black cats just ran under my ladder. ____________________

h That spell book is her's. ____________________

i Gremlins aren't real, but sometimes they seem to be around. ____________________

UNIT TEN

Grand designs

Focus

Adverbs; quotation marks: direct speech

Grammar in use

Great monuments rise **slowly** and **painfully**. Workmen began building the great German cathedral of Cologne in 1248. Some of their descendants were probably **still** working **there** when it was **finally** completed over 600 years later.

Working conditions were **usually very** dangerous in the past and workmen suffered terribly. They had barely enough to eat and were dogged by illness, injury and, **too** frequently, death. Because workmen were only seen as workers, their names were not recorded so their identities are lost to time.

Just sometimes we can glimpse their world—in expressions on the faces of Cathedral gargoyles and in graffiti scratched **deeply** into stone—along the lines of: *Otto was here.*

About grammar

Adverbs add meaning to (or **modify**) verbs, adjectives and other adverbs.

- **Adverbs often end in *ly***; for example, *slow***ly**, *painful***ly**. But there are many adverbs which do not; for example, *soon, always, never, sometimes, almost, here, there, far, much, most, still, twice* and *fast*.
- Adverbs usually tell us
  - » **how** the verb happens; for example, *rise* **slowly** *and* **painfully**/*scratched* **deeply**.
  - » **when** the verb happens; for example, **finally** *completed*/**still** *working*.
  - » **where** the verb happens; for example, *working* **there**.
  - » **how frequently** the verb happens; for example, *were* **usually**.
- Adverbs are used to add meaning to adjectives and other adverbs. They show us the **degree** (how much) of the adjective or adverb; for example, **very** *dangerous*/**too** *frequently.* Other adverbs of degree include *very, rather, quite, too, hardly, so, extremely, really, nearly, only, enough* and *just*.
- We can **compare** adverbs just as we can compare adjectives, using *more* and *most*, and *less* and *least*; for example, **slowly**, *more slowly, most slowly*/**painfully**, *less painfully, least painfully.*
- Note: avoid the **common error** of using an adjective where an adverb is needed. For example:
  They worked **bad**. (✗). *They worked* **badly**. (✓)
  He worked **good**. (✗). *He worked* **well**. (✓)
  They worked **slow**. (✗). *They worked* **slowly**. (✓)
  His work was **real** *good.* (✗). *His work was* **really** *good.* (✓)
- And one more! You can't place *very* **directly before a noun**; for example, *It was* **very** *fun.* (✗). You need to use an adjective; for example, *It was* **great** *fun.* (✓)

Boost your grammar skills

1 Underline the **adverbs** and circle the verbs they modify.

For example: The old tower was quickly (demolished) to make way for the new one.

a The top of the Pearl Tower in Shanghai is usually shrouded in cloud.

b London's thousand-year-old White Tower gleams brightly in the morning light.

c Kuala Lumpur's Petronas Towers are cleverly linked by high walkways.

d Italy's Tower of Pisa has been slowly subsiding on one side for centuries.

e Sydney's Centrepoint Tower always provides spectacular views.

2 Insert an appropriate **adverb** into each sentence.

easily	now	sometimes	regularly	originally

a High-rise buildings ________________ sway if the wind is very strong.

b Mexico City was built over an old lake bed and ________________ it is quietly sinking.

c The bridge was ________________ planned as a suspension bridge.

d The Olympic stadium is ________________ used for international competitions.

e The Eiffel Tower is perhaps the most ________________ recognised structure in the world.

3 What do the underlined **adverbs** tell us about the verb in these sentences?

For example: The demolished building collapsed slowly in a cloud of dust. how

a German castles on the Rhine were there to control river trade. ____________

b Victoria's Westgate Bridge was once the site of a construction tragedy. ____________

c San Francisco's Golden Gate Bridge is a cleverly designed suspension bridge. ____________

d Japan's ancient stone castles were often sited on hill tops. ____________

e Fog makes Sydney Harbour bridge invisible occasionally. ____________

4 Underline any **adverbs** in Penny's description of her visit to the Yellow Crane Tower. (Hint: there are twelve.) Remember: they don't always end in *ly*.

> It was quite tiring climbing the hill to the Tower, but when we got there the view was absolutely spectacular. We could see the Yangtze River winding slowly across the plain, the carefully tended farms and the city in the distance. However, it was the Yellow Crane Tower itself that I most enjoyed. I loved the highly polished timber floors and the balconies roofed over with yellow ceramic tiles. I loved its unexpectedly cool interior, the faintly whispering breeze under its curved eaves and, especially, the enormously tall red-lacquered pillars that have stood there for centuries.

5 Tick (✔) the correct sentence in each pair. (Hint: look for the correct **adverb**.)

a **i** That was very fun. ____ **ii** That was terrific fun. ____

b **i** The team works together good. ____ **ii** The team work together well. ____

c **i** The building went up quickly. ____ **ii** The building went up quick. ____

d **i** The climb is really hard. ____ **ii** The climb is real hard. ____

e **i** Look real slow and careful. ____ **ii** Look really slowly and carefully. ____

6 All the **adverbs** have been omitted from this advertisement. Write an appropriate adverb from this list in each gap.

romantically	very	just	bravely	lazily

See yourself ____________ swimming among tropical fish? ____________ leaping off a cliff and bouncing back ____________ before you hit the ground? Dining ____________ in the moonlight? Book now—six glorious days on your ____________ own tropical island for a mere $900.

7 Underline all the **adverbs** in this text that do not end in *ly*. (**Tip**: there are nine altogether and two occur side by side.)

While I was waiting to climb the Sydney Harbour Bridge, I was rather scared and was very glad my elder brother had come with me. He's an engineering student and knows quite a lot about bridge construction. If he kept talking while we were climbing, I might not look down and see the green water far below. Soon we were on our way. It was a long way to the top and I started to puff halfway but it was well worth the climb. The view from the arch was spectacular.

8 Underline any noun used as an **adverb** in these sentences.

a Construction will begin tomorrow.

b Yesterday the concrete foundations were laid.

c If all teams cooperate today, the job will be finished.

d The new bridge lights will be switched on tonight.

Punctuation in use

It was a cold wet day and the Henry children were bored. **'Here, see what you can make with these,'** their father said as he tipped two large packets of matchsticks on the table. Immediately they cheered up.

'Let's make a farmyard to hold all my plastic farm animals,' shouted Ben.

Tom overruled him. 'Nah, we should build a railway station beside the train set tracks.'

'Trains are so yesterday,' wailed Clare. 'Why can't we build a castle?'

About punctuation

- **Direct speech** refers to the actual words spoken by someone.
- Direct speech is enclosed by **quotation marks** (also called inverted commas); for example, **'Here, see what you can make with these,'** *their father said.*
- The **end punctuation** should also be enclosed in the quotation marks; for example, **'Why can't we build a castle?'** (The question mark is enclosed.)
- However, if the direct speech ends in a full stop, but is followed by words such as *he said* or *replied Susan*, a **comma** is used instead of a full stop; for example, **'Let's make a farmyard to hold all my plastic farm animals,'** *shouted Ben.*
- When we **interrupt direct speech** we close the inverted commas and open new ones to continue the quoted speech; for example, **'Trains are so yesterday,' wailed Clare. 'Why can't we build a castle?'**
- When a new speaker begins to talk we start a **new paragraph**.

Boost your punctuation skills

1 Enclose the **direct speech** in the sentences below in **quotation marks**.

- **a** Who designed the Eiffel Tower in Paris? asked Selma.
- **b** Did you know that London Bridge was demolished and rebuilt in America? Sam said.
- **c** What sort of road machine does your father drive? asked Peter.
- **d** Did you visit the Red Fort in Delhi while you were there? Mrs Harris enquired.
- **e** The tourist guide warned us: Don't enter the roped-off areas of the castle.

2 Put in the missing end punctuation in the **direct speech** examples below.

- **a** 'I love medieval castles__' Maria told her father.
- **b** 'How did people raise the giant statues on Easter Island__' asked the student.
- **c** The overseer shouted 'Pull__' and the workers hauled on the rope.
- **d** 'Jim drives huge ore trucks at the iron mine__' his brother said proudly.
- **e** 'Good grief__' Mrs Bindon exclaimed at the sight of the mud on their work clothes.

3 Edit the following text of a conversation. Put in the missing **quotation marks**.

- **a** What is this Taj we're supposed to be discussing? David wanted to know. I've been away all week and I don't know what we're talking about.
- **b** It's a mausoleum, a big above-ground tomb, in India, offered Lal.
- **c** And it's a memorial too, chimed in Jai. The Emperor Shah Jehan built it to honour his wife.
- **d** He must have loved her very much, sighed Amy. Is it a very beautiful memorial?
- **e** Tomorrow we'll be talking about the ruins of Petra said Mrs Hadad. Please read up and come prepared.

4 Mark with a square bracket ([) where each **new paragraph** should begin in this text.

> 'How did people warm those old European castles?' Fiona asked her history teacher. 'If they were built of stone they must have been very cold in winter.' 'Yes they were, Fiona. That's a good question. Can anyone tell us how they were heated?' 'I know, Sir,' Tom called out. 'They built a great big fire in every room.' 'But there were lots and lots of rooms,' objected William.

5 These examples of **direct speech** are correctly punctuated. True or false?

a 'Did Marcus see Canada from the top of Chicago's Sears Tower?' asked Peter. ____________

b Rome's aqueducts were an engineering marvel, Dr. Rose told the boys. ____________

c 'I want to visit Buckingham Palace when I grow up,' Lisa wrote. ____________

d 'How did masons fit those huge blocks of stones together?' we asked the guide. ____________

e Why are so many tall spires covered in copper sheeting? was the first question. ____________

6 Punctuate these correctly. Remember, book and film titles also need **quotation marks**.

a A reference book, Bridge Construction, lay on a table. Would you put it back on its shelf please, Elizabeth, the librarian said.

b The girls hired a movie called The Matrix, only to have Tom, say I've seen that.

c The protesters waved two kinds of banners, one saying Save our wilderness! and the other No more dams!

d Peter read the sign aloud: No object shall be thrown from this bridge. Penalty for infringement $280.

e Haul away! the groundsman shouted to the crane driver, The load's all secure.

7 Rewrite these indirect questions as **direct speech**. You need to think carefully about the actual words spoken, and start with these as in the example. (Note: you may have to change the tense of the verb and change or add a word.)

For example: Sue said that lightning had struck the hospital.
'Lightning struck the hospital,' said Sue.

a Colin asked us whether we were going to the new indoor pool.

____

____

b Head Office inquired what the likely completion date was?

____

____

c Hong Liu told us that the usual pagoda colours in China were red, green and gold.

____

____

d The architect reassured Mr Habib that all modern buildings use reinforced concrete.

____

____

UNIT ELEVEN

Having fun

Focus

Clauses and compound sentences; apostrophes of possession

Grammar in use

In the school holidays our family **went** camping. We camped in the bush beside a small creek near to the beach. The beach had a good surf so **it** was great for boogie-boarding.

For ten days we fished in the creek and fried our catch for lunch and dinner. We body-surfed, boogie-boarded and built sandcastles with our little cousins. A lot of the time we played beach volleyball.

We ran and jumped and tossed and caught and sometimes just collapsed with exhaustion. My cousin, Victor, **was** the tallest but he **wasn't** always the hardest to beat. That honour went to my brother, Liam. Liam was small enough to get under everyone's guard **so** he could snatch the ball for a quick flick over the rope. His shots always fell too short for anyone to return.

About grammar

- Sometimes a sentence has one verb; for example, *In the school holidays our family* **went** *camping*. This is called a **simple sentence**. (We first looked at simple sentences in Chapter 4.)
- A simple sentence consists of **one clause**—one unit of meaning with one verb.
- Sometimes we join two or more simple sentences together to make a longer sentence. This is called a **compound sentence**. (We looked at these very briefly in Chapter 4.)
- A compound sentence contains **two or more clauses** of equal importance. Each clause contains one verb and is independent—that is, it can stand alone and make sense; for example, *My cousin, Victor,* **was** *the tallest but he* **wasn't** *always the hardest to beat.*
- We join the two clauses in compound sentences with **coordinate conjunctions**: *and, but, yet, or, nor, then* and (sometimes) *so.*
- We often **leave out** the noun or pronoun in the second clause if it is **the same as** the one in the first clause; for example, *we* is omitted in the second clause in **For ten days we fished in the creek and fried our catch for lunch and dinner**.
- We often **replace the noun** in the first clause with a **pronoun** in the second; for example, *The beach had a good surf so* **it** *was great for boogie-boarding.*

Boost your grammar skills

1 Underline the **verbs** in each **sentence**.

a Peter goes walking on Long Neck Ridge.

b Helena climbed Mt Kosciusko last week.

c A triathlete cycles but he also runs and swims.

d A chess player thinks then makes a move.

2 Write *S* for **simple sentence** or *C* for **compound sentence** for the sentences below. (Hint: don't rely on the length of the sentence—count the verbs.)

a Ocean sailing is a rich man's sport. ____

b Bungee jumping is exhilarating but it is also terrifying. ____

c Snorkelling can open a new underwater world to the adventurous. ____

d Playing the bagpipes is not easy at first, but with practice it can become a joy. ____

e Sand boarding is an increasingly popular pastime with young people. ____

3 Underline the **independent clauses** in each sentence. There could be one, two or three.

a Irene enjoys sewing and she especially enjoys embroidery.

b Paul collects foreign stamps but Charlie and Craig collect football cards.

c The girls played hard until the final whistle but they were beaten in the end.

d Acting appeals to many people but Heidi wanted to be theatrical lighting engineer.

e As a child Henry watched butterflies, then he graduated to collecting them and finally he became an entomologist with butterfly expertise.

f Penny learned to knit but that was not enough for her and she learned to crochet too.

4 Join the sentences to make **compound sentences** using one of these conjunctions.

and	so	but	or

a Archery looks easy. It takes tremendous strength to draw back the bow.

____

b Long boards were once popular. Modern short boards are better for surfing.

____

c Sharks swim close to the shore in summer. Wise surfers stay behind the shark net.

____

d My mother was not keen on my playing football. She suggested I play cricket or tennis.

____

e The Browns Flat team were bigger. Our team was faster. We won.

____

f Do you like doing extreme sports? Do you prefer to watch them on TV?

____

5 Change the underlined conjunctions to help these **compound sentences** make better sense.

a That motor launch is fast <u>and</u> that one with twin outboards is faster. ________

b It's fun to ride bareback <u>so</u> stirrups, saddles and hard hats make it safer. ________

c Stilt walking was popular in the Middle Ages <u>and</u> very few people can do it today. ________

d Will it rain this afternoon for sport <u>and</u> will it be fine? ________

e Do you know the rules for touch footy <u>so</u> would you rather play brandings? ________

6 Underline all the **coordinate conjunctions**.

> Playing an instrument can be very rewarding but it is hard work. It takes much practice and it takes even more dedication. It is a personal pursuit but it can give an audience a lot of pleasure. Most musicians prefer one instrument or at most they play two.

7 The following text is a string of **simple sentences** but it has no full stops. Put full stops where needed to break into simple sentences. Choose at least two simple sentences that could be joined into a **compound sentence** and then write it on the answer lines. (Think about the meaning—some sentences would be better joined than others.) There is more than one way to do this.

> The table game of mahjong began in China it is played with a set of 136 small rectangular tiles each tile carries a symbol or a Chinese writing character four players each draw 13 tiles the object of the game is to build a city wall with these tiles the player who first exhausts the supply of tiles wins.

____

____

____

____

8 Make this recount flow more easily by combining some short sentences into **compound sentences**. Take out any repetitive nouns or pronouns and add **commas** where needed. There is more than one way to do this.

> Surfing is the greatest fun. You paddle out. You turn. You wait for a big wave to roll in. You catch it. You straighten out balancing your feet fore and aft. You ride your wave in. If you're lucky it will curl over you. You can ride across the underbelly of the wave inside the curl of its crest.

____

____

____

____

9 Correct these sentences by changing the **coordinate conjunction**.

a He didn't damage he bike but he shouldn't have to repair it.

b Backgammon is a board game because it's not very popular.

Punctuation in use

Rebecca's girls were unsure whether victory on the field would be theirs. Still, netball was their game and the **season's** score was in their favour so they had better just get their **team's** strategy planned, go out there and do battle with the Dragons. The **boys'** soccer team would be spectators.

First half went the Dragons' way but after a pep talk at halftime, the Ladybirds forced half a dozen penalties in as many minutes. **Charles's** voice shouted, "Go the Ladybirds!" and the **Ladybirds'** response was immediate—an outside ring goal followed by another from its bounce.

About punctuation

- **Apostrophes** (') are used to show **possession** of one noun or noun group by another; for example, *Rebecca***'s** *girls* → *girls of Rebecca.*
- Apostrophes of possession are always **placed after the last letter of the possessing noun**, so the best way to work out where to put the apostrophe is to ask *Who does the owning?* In this example, *Who owns the girls?*, the answer is *Rebecca*, so the apostrophe goes directly after the word *Rebecca*.
- If you have trouble with this rule, you can use the following rules instead.
  - » For **singular possessing nouns** the apostrophe goes **before the** ***s***; for example, *the season***'s** *score (the score of the season)/their team***'s** *strategy (the strategy of the team).*
  - » For **plural possessing nouns** the apostrophe goes **after the** ***s***; for example, *boys***'** *soccer team (soccer team of the boys)/Ladybirds***'** *response (response of the Ladybirds).*
  - » When the possessing noun is **irregular** like *women, men* and *children* the apostrophe goes **before the** ***s***; for example, *women***'s** *victory (victory of the women).*
- Note: a singular noun ending in *s* can show **possession** in two ways: *Charles' voice* or *Charles***'s** *voice* (The latter is recommended.)
- Remember:
  - » Possessive pronouns do **not** need apostrophes; for example, *theirs, its* and *hers.*
  - » Not all words that end in *s* take an apostrophe, only those that **own the following word**; for example, *John's house* and *Julie's cat* are correct. *Tomatoes' for sale* and *Apple's $2 a bag* are incorrect.

Boost your punctuation skills

1 Turn these phrases around so you can show **possession** with *'s*. The first one has been done for you.

a in the pocket of Hannah ______ in Hannah's pocket ______

b in the laboratory of Dr Hale ____________

c in the class of the girls ____________

d with the support of many people ____________

e into the black depths of the ocean ____________

f in the race of the men ____________

2 Add an **apostrophe** to the noun in possession of the underlined noun or noun group.

For example: The archer armguard is essential protection. archer's

a Her steel mesh mask protects a fencer nose from a rapier thrust. ____________

b A diver greatest danger is rising too fast and developing the bends. ____________

c His car inbuilt rigid steel frame protects the racing car driver. ____________

d Canada bobsled competitions are fast and furious. ____________

e The rower efforts were rewarded when they won the race. ____________

f The swimmer success in their relay pleased us all. ____________

3 Do the underlined words need an **apostrophe**? Circle either *yes* or *no*.

a The truck has jammed its gears. (yes/no)

b That computers memory capacity is huge. (yes/no)

c The student bodys dance proposal to the Principal was accepted. (yes/no)

d Carolines paintings are usually abstracts in shades of blue. (yes/no)

e The trophy was theirs to keep. (yes/no)

4 Casey doesn't know how to use apostrophes. Add any necessary **apostrophes** and write the corrected words in the spaces. The first one has been done for you.

My fathers father's amazing inventions all happen in the back shed. The old bird cages ____________ base became the roof of Marcies ____________ new rabbit hutch. The boys ____________ bikes have been rebuilt for mountain bike work down in Dads ____________ shed. Mr Harris ____________ car lost an exhaust pipe so Dad found a replacement for it from the sheds ____________ bottomless chest of spares.

5 Keiran has made mistakes with his **apostrophes**. Write the correction on the line.

a Mens' hockey is one of the fastest games in the world. ____________

b Pete's skateboard needs new wheels and Chriss' could do with a coat of paint. ____________

c An ice rinks' surface is so slippery many spend more time sitting then skating. ____________

d The girl's rap dancing was great, but they did not win the competition. ____________

e Each choirs' place on the program related to a performance time slot. ____________

6 Which advertisements misuse the **apostrophe**? Cross (✗) them in the spaces.

a Bananas' $1/kg. Today only! ____

b Tomato's $2 a box! ____

c Bob Kane's Tyre Mart ____

d Sale! Early bird get's the worm! ____

e Yamaha—Music's grandest piano ____

f Stonewashed jeans' sale ____

g Wok's that rock! ____

h Bill's Books and Magazines ____

UNIT TWELVE

12 A world of colour

Focus

Clauses and complex sentences; commas (5)

Grammar in use

The great river slides westward **as** the sun rises. The early light catches an egret preening on a log. **The river is wide here at the bend where it sweeps under tall red cliffs.**

A shag, **who looks for all the world like an undertaker**, hangs his black wings out to dry. Below the surface a toad-mouthed Murray cod hangs in the slack water of the lee bank, while a blue heron stalks the shallows.

A screech of cockatoos greets the sun as it crests the mighty red gums on the bank. An electric blue kingfisher flits across the water's surface and raises a shower of droplets **that** fracture into rainbows. It's going to be another long golden day on the river.

About grammar

- Sometimes an idea is too complex to be expressed in a simple or compound sentence. In these cases we need **complex sentences**.
- A complex sentence contains an **independent main clause** with the main piece of information, and one or more **dependent** (or subordinate) **clauses** which contain extra detail; for example, **The river is wide here at the bend** (independent) **where it sweeps under tall red cliffs** (dependent).
- Remember: the independent clause is the **important part** of the sentence. The dependent clause gives **extra information**.
- Dependent clauses which add information about the verb in the main clause are often called **adverbial clauses** (because they act like adverbs). They are joined to the main clause with subordinate conjunctions; for example, *when, where, as, if, although, while, since, until, whenever, because* and *unless*, such as in *The great river slides westward* **as** *the sun rises.*
- Dependent clauses which add information about the noun in the main clause are often called **adjectival clauses** (because they act like adjectives). They are joined to the main clause with relative pronouns; for example, *which, that, who, whom* and *whose*, such as in *An electric blue kingfisher … raises a shower of droplets* **that** *fracture into rainbows.*
- Dependent clauses can come **before** a main clause or **follow** a main clause, or even occur in the middle of a main clause; for example, *A shag,* **who looks for all the world like an undertaker**, *hangs his black wings out to dry.*

Boost your grammar skills

1 Connect these **main clauses** to their **dependent clauses** with a line.

a Firefighters wear yellow,	although I missed the first bus.
b We cannot go bushwalking	who must protect their young
c I arrived on time	when viewed underwater
d Elise kayaks on the river	because it is going to rain.
e Mr Harris, ________, is very ill.	which is a highly visible colour.
f Hen birds, ________, have plain feathers.	whenever she has time.
g Coral reefs, ________, glow with colour.	who was to lead our bush excursion

2 Choose the correct conjunction to link the **main** and **dependent clauses** in these sentences.

when	which	that	where	whose

a Ireland, ________________ is called The Emerald Isle, is also called the Land of Saints and Scholars.

b The Andes Mountains include many volcanoes ________________ are still active.

c India, ________________ northern border is The Himalayas, has green jungles and yellow beaches.

d New Zealand's south island, ________________ living glaciers still flow, is a lovely wilderness.

e El Nino, ________________ it brings drought to Australia, brings floods to Chile.

3 Underline the **dependent clauses** in these sentences.

For example: Antarctica is a cruelly cold white land <u>that has a permanently frozen surface.</u>

a The forests of North America glow red and gold when autumn closes in.

b Central Australia desert gums are multicoloured as Namatjira's paintings show.

c The grasslands of the Serengeti, where wild creatures roam in vast herds, are yellow.

d The Blue Mountains, which lie west of Sydney, are known for their blue eucalyptus haze and rugged beauty.

e White houses line cobbled streets which run down to the shores of the blue Aegean.

4 Write an **adverbial clause** in the space to complete each sentence. The first one has been done for you.

a Stacey wants to be a deep-sea diver when she grows up.

b ______________________________ Samantha was seasick.

c They waited for an hour after lunch ______________________________

d ______________________________ there is a pretty green valley.

e ______________________________ you must not be afraid of heights.

f We heard loud thunder ______________________________

5 Write an **adjectival clause** in the space to complete each sentence. The first one has been done for you.

a Mr Jackson was driving the bus that got lost in the desert.

b Uluru, ______________________________,
is a spectacular sight from the air.

c We followed the track

____

d They were blinded by the blizzard

____

e We lay in our swags and looked at the stars

____

6 Write *S* for sentence beside the **independent clauses** and *D* for dependent beside the **dependent clauses**.

a A full moon is bright yellow. __________

b While I was sleeping __________

c whose new backpack was stolen __________

d Although it was grey and cold __________

e The sun blazed bronze and hot. __________

7 Underline the three **dependent clauses** in this piece of prose poetry.

> Quartz-spark stars catch the light of a pale moon like the tiny mirrors that gleam from Indian veiling. The Southern Cross shines cold as glass, as it did when the Nunnawal first sang its Dreamtime story to wide-eyed children.
>
> (from 'The Galled Tree' by Jane Baker)

8 Fill the spaces in Alice's description with these **subordinate** and **coordinate conjunctions**.

so	where	when	and	which

Outside my room a gum tree stands __________ it has stood for at least a hundred years. It is taller than the chimney of our house __________ is at least three metres around its trunk. Its bark, __________ cracks and peels off every autumn, reveals new silver-white bark. Over the year this new bark turns various colours from pink through to grey. __________ it rains the bark shines pink, grey, yellow, green and mauve __________ it almost looks like a painting.

Punctuation in use

Imagine for a moment you are in the Amazonian jungle. **As the light filters down through the dark tree canopy**, you see some extraordinary creatures. Shy sloths, **who move so slowly you'd think they were asleep,** slumber high up in the tree tops. There are colours all around, but if you look very carefully, you might pick out the brilliant plumage of the scarlet macaw. Agouti, **which look like little sharp-snouted pigs,** snuffle through leaf litter in search of fallen nuts and fruit. **If you are very lucky,** you might see a jaguar sprawled on a branch in his elegantly spotted coat, which is perfectly camouflaged in the dappled light.

About punctuation

- We first looked at using **commas** in long sentences in Chapter 6. Because **complex sentences** can be long, they often need commas to help make the meaning clear.
- We often use commas to **separate adverbial clauses** at the start of sentences; for example, **As the light filters down through the dark tree canopy,** *you see some extraordinary creatures.*/**If you are very lucky,** *you might see a jaguar …*
- We also use commas to **mark a dependent clause** within a sentence, when that clause adds extra but non-essential information; for example, *Shy sloths,* **who move so slowly you'd think they were asleep**, *slumber high up in the tree tops./Agouti,* **which look like little sharp-snouted pigs**, *snuffle through leaf litter.*
- Remember: we also use commas to **separate two clauses in a compound sentence**, especially if the sentence is quite long. (See Chapter 6.)

Boost your punctuation skills

1 Use **commas** to separate the **adverbial clauses** in these sentences.

For example: As caterpillars grow, they shed their skins several times.

a When the sun sets over the horizon the night creatures of the desert venture out.

b Because the sloth has bad hearing and bad sight it has to rely on smell and touch.

c Although the toucan's large yellow bill looks frightening to predators it is actually of little use in a fight.

d While the clownfish might look pretty with its orange and white stripes it is actually covered in slime.

e When a bee finds flowers with nectar it tells the other bees through dancing and smell signs.

2 Use **commas** to separate the **dependent clause** inside the **main clause** in these sentences.

For example: Rock pools, when the tide is out, can hold the deadly blue-ringed octopus.

a Deserts which we think of as yellow can be red, grey, brown and even black.

b Lake Eyre which is usually white becomes a blue lake when flooded.

c At first light after high tide has washed it clean the beach always looks serene.

d Australia's scarlet waratah which grows in cool misty valleys is cousin to the protea.

e Sydney Harbour's shores after a storm has raged through are littered with shells.

3 Tick (✔) correctly punctuated sentences and cross (✘) those that are incorrect.

a Sydney Harbour which is Australia's premier port is a busy colourful harbour. ____

b Tasmania's Styx Valley, when wreathed in mist, is breathtakingly beautiful. ____

c West Australia's wildflowers after a rare shower has fallen bloom brilliantly. ____

d Moreton Bay fig trees, which are a favoured haunt of flying foxes, are dense and dark. ____

e A red kangaroo, although it may stand two metres tall, can easily disappear into the red landscape of the desert. ____

4 Put in all the **commas** Nguyen has forgotten in his hurry to write this letter.

> Dear Nathan,
>
> We are here in my grandmother's village where all my ancestors have lived for generations and I'm having a ball. Uncle Pham who's my Dad's oldest brother takes me fishing out on Halong Bay every morning. We row out at first light and drop our lines near one of the islands. Quickly we catch enough fish for breakfast and hurry home. If we're really lucky Grandma will be waiting to grill them up for us. It will be good to get back home to catch up with what's been happening while I've been away but I'll never forget this trip.

5 Erin uses far too many commas. Put a cross (✘) next to any unnecessary **commas** in this story. Use your own judgement as well as the rules you have learnt.

> In our back garden, which is very steep, and has lots of rockeries, I have a pet blue-tongued lizard. He's not really a pet, I know, but he behaves like one. He's about as long as a ruler, and quite fat. His tongue really is blue, as his name suggests, and his eyes are bright black, and curious. His body is striped, vividly, in yellow and brown, although most other blue tongues, I have seen, are shades of blue grey. He lives in a crevice, but, he sleeps on top of a boulder, during the day if the sun is out.

6 Fill in the missing **commas**.

a If you want to be precise blue black is properly called barathea blue.

b Wherever she goes and whenever she travels she always wears red.

c Although we call him Bluey as do his parents Peter actually has red hair.

d As a storm approached over the sea an eerie green light washed the beach.

e A peahen is quite dowdy despite the fact that her mate is so vividly turquoise.

f Brown snakes which are venomous creatures are slim and elegant.

g Quolls which are small spotted carnivores live in Australia's forests.

h Wallabies even though they are small can leap up steep cliffsides with ease.

Revision Test 3

Grammar

Shade one circle to show the correct answer.

1 Which line contains only adjectives?

- ◯ fish, balance, hammer, hard, rod
- ◯ large, tiny, purple, heavy, unexpected
- ◯ here, there, always, red, green
- ◯ climb, fence, ugly, high, gone

2 Which sentence correctly underlines the adjective?

- ◯ The Eiffel Tower is the tallest building in Paris.
- ◯ The Eiffel Tower is the tallest building in Paris.
- ◯ The Eiffel Tower is the tallest building in Paris.
- ◯ The Eiffel Tower is the tallest building in Paris.

In questions 3–6, which sentence is correct?

3

- ◯ Tracey was the baddest Cyclone to strike Australia.
- ◯ Tracey was the worse cyclone to strike Australia.
- ◯ Tracey was the worst cyclone to strike Australia.
- ◯ Tracey was the most bad cyclone to strike Australia.

4

- ◯ Eddie is carefuller than Tom.
- ◯ Eddie is more careful than Tom.
- ◯ Eddie is carefuller like Tom.
- ◯ Eddie is more carefuller than Tom.

5

- ◯ Shelley was real careful.
- ◯ Shelley was really careful.

6

- ◯ The boys completed the task quick.
- ◯ The boys completed the task quicker.
- ◯ The boys completed the task quickly.
- ◯ The boys completed the task quickest.

7 Which adverb correctly completes this sentence?

Potatoes ________________ came from South America but are now grown all over the world.

- ◯ finally
- ◯ lastly
- ◯ originally
- ◯ usually

8 Which line contains only adverbs?

- happy, excited, cheerfully, that, then
- leave, around, scarlet, friend, dog
- unless, useful, place, time, never
- here, anxiously, silently, really, always

In questions 9–11, which conjunction joins the two sentences?

9 We like swimming. We like skateboarding more.

- and
- but
- so
- then

10 We played billiards. It was too wet to go riding.

- until
- because
- unless
- although

11 The Magpies won't make the finals. They think up new strategy.

- because
- although
- unless
- since

12 Which conjunction correctly completes this sentence?

________________ Kyra wins the semi-finals, she will qualify for the national competition.

- As
- If
- Unless
- While

In questions 13–14, how many clauses are in each sentence?

13 Last week we had our exams, we had the regional swimming carnival and we had the school fete.

- one
- two
- three
- four

14 The Lennox Bridge which is the oldest bridge on mainland Australia is built of sandstone.

- one
- two
- three
- four

15 Which sentence correctly underlines the adverb?

- The great river slowly made its winding way to the sea.
- The great river slowly made its winding way to the sea.
- The great river slowly made its winding way to the sea.
- The great river slowly made its winding way to the sea.

16 In which sentence is the main clause underlined?

- The weird Min Min light can be frightening when it is first encountered.
- The weird Min Min light can be frightening when it is first encountered.
- The weird Min Min light can be frightening when it is first encountered.
- The weird Min Min light can be frightening when it is first encountered.

Punctuation

In questions 1–4, which contraction is written correctly?

1
- isnt
- ‘isnt
- i’snt
- isn’t

2
- wer’ent
- weren’t
- were’nt
- werent’

3
- haven’t
- hav’ent
- have’nt
- havent’

4
- should of
- should’ve
- should’have
- should’of

5 Which word correctly fills the gap in this sentence?

Some countries hold ancient treasures even though they were never ______________ to keep.

- there’s
- theirs’
- theirs
- their’s

6 Which phrase is correctly punctuated?

- Harveys’ house plan
- Harveys house plan
- Harvey’s house plan

In questions 7–15, which sentence is correctly punctuated?

7
- Stop, drop and crawl said the fireman when he told the children about fire safety.
- Stop, drop and crawl, said the fireman when he told the children about fire safety.
- ‘Stop, drop and crawl,’ said the fireman when he told the children about ‘fire safety’.
- ‘Stop, drop and crawl,’ said the fireman when he told the children about fire safety.

8
- ‘We could have won’ said Kyle, ‘What do you think, Joe?’
- ‘We could have won,’ said Kyle. ‘What do you think, Joe?’
- ‘We could have won,’ said Kyle, ‘What do you think, Joe’?
- ‘We could have won,’ said Kyle. ‘What do you think, Joe’?

9
- ◯ In which state is the Westgate Bridge? asked James.
- ◯ 'In which state is the Westgate Bridge?' asked James.
- ◯ 'In which state is the Westgate Bridge' asked James.
- ◯ 'In which state is the Westgate Bridge,' asked James.

10
- ◯ Penny Lewis's house is built of mud bricks.
- ◯ Penny Lewiss' house is built of mud bricks.
- ◯ Penny Lewis house is built of mud bricks.

11
- ◯ My next door neighbours have just moved to Queensland.
- ◯ My next door neighbour's have just moved to Queensland.
- ◯ My next door neighbours' have just moved to Queensland.
- ◯ My next door' neighbours have just moved to Queensland.

12
- ◯ Both boys' tents were damaged by the hailstorm.
- ◯ Both boys's tents were damaged by the hailstorm.
- ◯ Both boy's tents were damaged by the hailstorm.
- ◯ Both boys tents were damaged by the hailstorm.

13
- ◯ Before the girls started on their long trek they left, all their trip details with the police.
- ◯ Before the girls started on their long trek they left all their trip details with the police.
- ◯ Before the girls started, on their long trek they left all their trip details with the police.
- ◯ Before the girls started on their long trek, they left all their trip details with the police.

14
- ◯ Hannah Gilmore who knows a lot about gardening, reckons I should plant a lemon tree.
- ◯ Hannah Gilmore who knows a lot about gardening reckons I should plant a lemon tree.
- ◯ Hannah Gilmore, who knows a lot about gardening, reckons I should plant a lemon tree.
- ◯ Hannah Gilmore, who knows a lot about gardening reckons I should plant a lemon tree.

15
- ◯ If you really want to go out take a raincoat.
- ◯ If you really want to go out, take a raincoat.

16 Where does the comma go?

The boy looked ◯ very calm ◯ and composed at first ◯ but then his face crumpled ◯ up in pain.

UNIT THIRTEEN

Ambitions and adventures

Focus

Modality; dashes and brackets

Grammar in use

Last week on our class website we asked about your career goals. Here are some responses:

I **really** want to be an astronomer. It would be cool to discover a new planet or star! (Carla)

I **will** be a drummer. It's the only thing I want to do. (Kai)

I **would** like to be a professional footballer and play for Australia. (Vijay)

I'll **probably** be a doctor like my mum. I **certainly** want to work in medicine. (Will)

I'd like to be a singer but it's **unlikely** I guess. (Hannah)

I'll **definitely** work in the open air—**maybe** as a park ranger or a bush care worker. (Jeb)

Not sure yet. I **guess** I **could** be a pilot or maybe even a skydiver. (Dan)

- Words like **really**, **will**, **would**, **probably**, **certainly**, **unlikely**, **definitely**, **maybe**, **guess** and **could** allow us to express how certain we feel about what we are saying. This aspect of language is called **modality**.
- Useful words and expressions include
  - **modal verbs**; for example, *could, might, may, have to, must, ought to, should, can, need to, shall, will* and *would*.
  - some **nouns**; for example, *likelihood, possibility, probability* and *certainty*.
  - some **adjectives**; for example, *possible, probable, likely, unlikely, certain* and *sure*.
  - some **adverbs**; for example, *possibly, definitely, surely, perhaps, sometimes, always* and *never*.
  - some **phrases**; for example, *I guess, I suppose, I think* and *to some extent*.
- These modal words and expressions also allow us to be softer and more polite when we want to **make a suggestion** or **express our opinions and beliefs**; for example, we can say (going from least to most polite) *Work harder* or *You must work harder* or *Maybe you should work harder* or *Possibly you should think about working a little harder*.
- **High modality** means certain or strong feeling; for example, *must, definitely, never*. **Low modality** means uncertain or weak feeling; for example, *may, perhaps*.

Boost your grammar skills

1 Look back at the student career goals on the previous page.

- **a** Which student is most certain about the future? Which **modal** words or expressions convey this?

  ____

  ____

- **b** Which is the least certain? Which **modal** words or expressions convey this?

  ____

  ____

2 Underline any **modal** words or expressions you find in these sentences.

- **a** It might rain this afternoon so abseiling would not be wise.
- **b** Cliff faces can be very slippery and wet ropes can fray very fast in those conditions.
- **c** Deep sea divers must rise very slowly to the surface. Too rapid an ascent can cause the bends, which can be fatal.
- **d** Bushwalkers should leave a plan of their walk and firm times for return with relatives.
- **e** Funnel-web spider venom can kill so victims must definitely go to hospital for antivenin treatment.

3 Write *H* for high or *L* for low to describe the **modality** level in these sentence pairs. Underline the **modal** words and expressions you find. Remember: high modality means certain and low modality means uncertain.

- **a i** To be a wreck diver you must complete several levels of training. ________
  - **ii** To be a wreck diver I think you need to complete several levels of training. ________
- **b i** You may climb that rope ladder to the next level. ________
  - **ii** You must climb that rope ladder to the next level. ________
- **c i** Shona will earn her pilot's wings by the end of June. ________
  - **ii** Perhaps Shona could earn her pilot's wings by the end of June. ________
- **d i** Charles could possibly learn piano and violin. ________
  - **ii** Charles ought to learn piano and violin. ________
- **e i** Jet skiers have to wear lifejackets. ________
  - **ii** Jet skiers should probably wear lifejackets. ________

4 Put these sentences in order from the strongest, **most certain** expression of feeling (write *1*) to the weakest, **least certain** (write *5*).

- **a** Shona will certainly fulfil her dreams before she is 30. ________
- **b** Shona will possibly fulfil her dreams before she is 30. ________
- **c** Shona will probably fulfil her dreams before she is 30. ________
- **d** Shona will most definitely fulfil her dreams before she is 30. ________
- **e** Maybe Shona could fulfil her dreams before she is 30. ________

5 **Modality** allows us to soften our message to make it more polite. Which one in the following pairs are the softest or most polite? Tick (✔) one.

a Board notice

i _____ Team meeting 11am on the dot. Bring your own gear and don't be late.

ii _____ Team meeting 11 am. Please bring your gear with you. Your punctuality would be appreciated.

b Text message

i _____ I don't think it was such a good idea to tell Carey.

ii _____ You shouldn't have told Carey.

c Email

i _____ Tell me if you're interested.

ii _____ Could you let me know if you think you might be interested?

6 Write these **modal** words in appropriate gaps in Cathy's recount. There is more than one possible answer in some cases.

could	probably	might	could	may	possibility	possible	will

We went caving at the weekend. Once inside the cave, we followed a small underground stream into a large chamber that looked as if it ____________________ have once been the reception hall of a king. As we looked around we ____________________ hear a rustling above our heads. It ____________________ have been bats but we ____________________ never know because we fled back until it was ____________________ to see the clean blue sky above. My father thinks it was ____________________ just a drift of leaves on ledges near the roof of the cave, but the ____________________ of bats flapping round us in the dark ____________________ well see us taking up abseiling instead.

7 Write this information in **a) high modality** and then **b) low modality**.

> Band practice for Eisteddfod after school Monday, Wednesday and Friday and all day Saturday. Bring own lunch on Saturday as well as instrument.

a ____

____

____

____

____

____

b ____

____

____

____

____

____

Punctuation in use

Angie stomped up the stairs and**—her face like thunder—**slammed the door of her room. She sat down to tackle her homework and**—ooh, her brother was so mean—**opened her book. She started to read:

Jessica Watson ***(born 18 May, 1993)*** *became the youngest person to sail non-stop and unassisted around the world. Her route did not meet the requirements of the World Sail Speed Record Council* ***(WSSRC)*** *and so her record remains unofficial. Departing from Sydney on October 18, 2009, Jessica crossed three oceans* ***(the Pacific, Atlantic and Indian)*** *and returned seven months later, just days before her 17th birthday.*

Angie forgot her own problems and—her attention totally captured—read on.

About punctuation

- We use **dashes** (—) and **brackets ( )** to add an extra piece of information to a sentence.
- Brackets are also called **parentheses**. They always come in pairs no matter where they are in a sentence; for example, *Jessica Watson (***born 18 May, 1993***)* not *Jessica Watson (born 18 May, 1993.*
- Brackets are **more formal** than dashes. You are more likely to use dashes in an email or a short story. In an essay or report you would be more likely to use brackets.
- Dashes can be used generally to **set apart extra information**, but often they enclose expressions of feeling about the topic of the sentence; for example, *and***—her face like thunder—***slammed the door*. They can also show a sudden change of direction in the sentence; for example, *She sat down to tackle her homework and***—ooh, her mother was so mean—***opened her book.*
- Brackets are often used to give a **definition**, an **explanation**, an **abbreviation** or an **example**; for example, *the requirements of the World Sail Speed Record Council* **(WSSRC)**/ *three oceans* **(the Pacific, Atlantic and Indian)**.
- Take care **not to use too many** brackets or dashes. If you do, your writing will be difficult to understand. Often a comma will do the job just as well.

Boost your punctuation skills

1 Put **brackets** where needed in these sentences.

a Jessica's boat measured 10.23 metres 33.6 feet.

b Sand skiing also called dune busting is a fun sport.

c Hang-gliding one of the more extreme sports has many followers.

d Gliding flying without power is an exhilarating experience.

e A typical skydive involves jumping from an aircraft usually an aeroplane but sometimes a helicopter or balloon.

f Competition fencing fighting with slim swords called foils is a demanding sport.

g Adventurers are now safer because of GPS global positioning system.

2 Write one of the comments below in each sentence, using **dashes** to mark them.

Ouch	not to mention luck
mmm, just smell that exhaust	don't just pat the ball
and a very good one	silly boy

a Whack it ______________________________ whack it!

b He's a helicopter pilot ______________________________ and he loves it.

c I love this speedway ______________________________.

d Keeping birds is fun but ______________________________ you must protect your fingers.

e Bike racing needs stamina ______________________________ if you are to win the Tour de France.

f Anthony ______________________________ lost his shoe in the creek while feeling for yabbies.

3 **a** Simon's talk is to be printed in the school magazine. Edit it for missing **dashes**.

> On our Year 8 school camp we did all sorts of adventurous things. One thing we did the best thing we did was build a flying fox. Our camp supervisor take a bow Mr. Loukakis told us what to do and we built it ourselves. When it was finished we all had a turn flying between the trees at either end. We built it over a waterhole so some of us accidentally like on purpose accidentally fell from the ropes into the water. It was great fun.

b Why do you think **dashes** are better than **brackets** in the text above?

____

____

4 Tick (✔) the correctly punctuated sentences and cross (✘) the incorrect ones.

a Paul—the smallest and skinniest of the runners—led from the start. ________

b Green Phantom is in the lead, Galway close behind—oh dear—Galway's fallen. ________

c Polo an equestrian sport originating in Tibet is played with a ball. ________

d Archery once a means of making war is now a popular sport. ________

e If I was a boy and I'm glad I'm not I'd play Australian Rules football. ________

f Gliding is an exhilarating pastime (although an expensive hobby to pursue). ________

5 Underline the words you would enclose in **dashes** in this story extract.

> Elise clung to the cliff. She had to swallow the taste of fear as she stretched upwards to a small hole that could serve as her next climbing grip. Spiders liked little holes too and she heaven help her was scared witless of spiders. Fortunately the hole was unoccupied. Elise gripped firmly with her right hand, and then wedged her left foot into a narrow rock chimney that miraculously ran all the way to the cliff top. She looked upwards and saw no, surely it wasn't possible her faithful little dog, Patch. Now she knew she would be OK.

UNIT FOURTEEN

14 Heroes and heroines

Focus

Active and passive voice; indirect speech

Grammar in use

Florence Nightingale was a 19th century English woman, who worked as a nurse during the Crimean War. There **she saw** the appalling conditions under which wounded men were treated. Dressings were not changed. **Floors in operating rooms were not washed**. Men lay in filthy cots or on the floor until they died of their injuries.

Nightingale introduced absolute cleanliness. A proper toilet system was established. Operating tables were disinfected, dressings were changed frequently and **a regular nutritional diet was introduced**. Nightingale's reforms saved the lives of countless soldiers and became the norm for hospital care.

- Verbs can either be in the **active voice** or the **passive voice.**
- We use the active voice when we want to focus on the person or thing **doing the verb action**. We make that person/thing the subject of the sentence; for example, *There* **she saw** *the appalling conditions …*/**Nightingale introduced** *absolute cleanliness.*
- We use the passive voice when we want to focus on the person or thing **being acted upon**, or on the **process or action itself**. We make that person/thing the subject of the sentence; for example, **Floors in operating rooms were not washed**./**a regular nutritional diet was introduced**.
- The passive voice is useful when we **don't want or need to mention** the person/thing **doing the action or involved in the process**. In the above examples, we don't need to mention the individual nurses or doctors who carried out these reforms. Our focus is on the reforms.
- We use the active voice more than the passive in **narratives** and **recounts** because it is more direct and focuses on the people we are writing about.
- We use the passive voice more often in **essays**, **reports** and other **formal writing** because it allows us to focus on general processes rather than specific people and things.

Boost your grammar skills

1 In these sentence pairs, write *A* for sentences that use the **active voice** and *P* for ones that use the **passive voice**. The first pair has been done for you.

a **i** The nurse saved his life. A

ii His life was saved by the nurse. P

b **i** The policeman chased the thief. ____

ii The thief was chased by the policeman. ____

c **i** Maria was helped to her feet by the nurse. ____

ii The nurse helped Maria to her feet. ____

d **i** The children were cheered by the crowd. ____

ii The crowd cheered the children. ____

e **i** My father saved the life of a surfer. ____

ii A surfer's life was saved by my father. ____

f **i** He is well-known by all Australians. ____

ii All Australians know him well. ____

2 Underline the verbs and write **active** or **passive** beside each of these sentences. The first one has been done for you.

a A fireman rescued the child from the burning house. active

b Wounded soldiers at Gallipoli were saved by Simpson and his donkey. ________

c Remote area accidents are attended by Air Ambulance. ________

d Rev. John Flynn established Australia's Flying Doctor Service. ________

e Two children were pulled from the surf after being caught in a rip. ________

f He was awarded his bravery medal before the school assembly. ________

3 Complete these sentences in the **passive voice** with the appropriate verb from the list.

were rescued	was treated	were assisted	are fought	was cut out

a Bushfires ____________ by the brave members of the Rural Fire Service.

b The victims of the recent storm damage ____________ by the State Emergency Service.

c The stranded flood victims ____________ by helicopter.

d The boy bitten by a funnel web spider ____________ with antivenin.

e The trapped driver ____________ of his car.

4 Rewrite each sentence in the **passive voice** so that the focus is **not** on the person. The first one has been done for you.

a Marie Curie discovered Radium.

Radium was discovered by Marie Curie.

b Mahatma Ghandi taught the principle of non-violence.

____

____

____

c In 1863 President Abraham Lincoln abolished slavery in the United States.

____

____

____

d Caroline Chisholm protected working girls in early New South Wales.

____

____

____

e Charles Babbage, an English inventor, designed the first computer.

____

____

____

5 Most recounts are written in the **active voice**, but sometimes the **passive** is needed. Look at Kai's recount and underline the two places where he uses the passive. For each one, decide if the use of the passive was suitable.

> We all saw the car hurtling down the hill into the river. It sank almost instantly and the driver was trapped. Harry called the police on his mobile but then we saw a boy diving into the river. Inside two minutes the boy emerged with a man in his arms. He quickly applied CPR and fortunately the man recovered. The ambulance was seen arriving minutes later.

1st passive: ______________________ **2nd passive:** ______________________

6 Most reports make some use of the **passive voice**. The report below uses both active and passive. Choose from the verbs below to complete the report.

decided	fought	did not live	was waged	was handed down	be recognised

Eddie Koiki Mabo was born in 1936 in the Murray Islands of the Torres Straits. Eddie ______________________ for his people's ownership of their Murray Islands to ______________________ by the Courts of Australia. The battle ______________________ peacefully in meetings, the media and the courts. In 1992 the High Court of Australia ______________________ that title to the Murray Islands belonged to the people of the Murray Islands, Eddie Mabo's people. Sadly, Eddie ______________________ to hear this decision, dying five months before it ______________________ by the Court.

7 Complete this text in the appropriate **voice**.

The sewing machine ______________________ (invent) by Elias Howe. By its invention women ______________________ (free) from the drudgery of handstitching. A shirt could ______________________ (sewn) in two hours by machine but ______________________ (take) up to a week by hand.

Punctuation in use

"Where would I find something on Damien Parer, the war photographer?" asked Chris.

The librarian told him the biographies were over by the window and asked if he needed a particular book.

"No thanks, Mrs Blake. I'll just have a general look."

Chris searched the shelves but with no luck. Then he heard Mrs Blake call out that a book on war photography had just been returned.

About punctuation

- We looked at punctuating **direct speech** in Chapter 10. Remember: direct speech is the exact words someone says. Direct speech and its end punctuation are all enclosed in inverted commas; for example, **"Where would I find something on Damien Parer, the war photographer?"** *asked Chris.*
- However, we can also show our reader what someone has said by using **indirect speech**. Indirect speech is a report of what someone has said but not always the exact words; for example, **The librarian told him the biographies were over by the window**. (In this case the librarian's exact words were: "The biographies are over by the window.")
- Indirect speech **needs no inverted commas** and usually ends in a full stop.
- **Conversation** can be written as direct or indirect speech, or as a mixture of both for interesting writing.
- Note: in indirect speech, you often change some words (especially **verbs**), **word order** and **end punctuation**; for example, *(she) asked if he needed a particular book.* (The librarian's exact words were: *"Do you need a particular book?")*

Boost your punctuation skills

1 Revise your knowledge of **direct speech** by correctly punctuating these sentences.

- **a** Did you know that three men have won two Victoria Crosses each asked Tom.
- **b** No I didn't. Tell me about them his brother replied.
- **c** Firefighters are the bravest people I know Geordie declared.
- **d** Sailors who climbed masts to set sails must have been very brave Elizabeth told her history class.
- **e** Peter looked up from his book to say My sister is a surf lifesaver. You can't get any braver than that.

2 Add the missing **punctuation** to these sentences. Some are direct speech and some are **indirect**.

- **a** Rosemary asked if anyone knew what really happened to the pilot, Amelia Earhart
- **b** Hey, you in the red jumper! That's not fair play, the referee shouted
- **c** Construction workers on high-rise buildings must have nerves of steel Steve said.

d Why do magpies swoop in Springtime Fatima asked

e Martha told Fatimah, magpies swoop to drive people away from babies in their nest

f His father said that he should face his fears. But I'm only six years old the boy cried.

3 **Punctuate** this reported conversation correctly.

> Let's go climbing today Alex said. Everyone except William thought it a great idea. William's excuse was that he had chores to do. That's all right Alex said we'll wait till you've done your chores. Then we'll go. There was a pause, and then William mumbled I don't really have chores to do. I'm just scared of heights. The others confessed that they had also been scared when they had first seen the climbing wall. Gino told him You'll love it once you get used to it William looked doubtful but agreed that he would at least go and watch.

4 Circle the correctly **punctuated** sentence.

a **i** 'Go away'! he shouted

ii Go away! he shouted.

iii 'Go away!' he shouted.

b **i** He wondered why he was late.

ii He wondered 'why he was late'.

iii He wondered why he was late?

c **i** The boys said that it had been a blast.

ii The boys said that 'it had been a blast.'

iii The boys said that it had been a blast.'

d **i** The teacher asked if Joe had won.

ii The teacher asked if Joe had won?

iii The teacher asked if 'Joe had won.'

5 Choose the correct **indirect speech** version of these direct speech examples.

a The doctor said, 'He is a very lucky boy.' (direct)

i The doctor said he was a very lucky boy.

ii The doctor said he is a very lucky boy.

b 'Will he help me?' the girl asked. (direct)

i The girl asked if he would help her.

ii The girl asked will he help her.

c What's your real name?' the teacher asked him. (direct)

i The teacher asked him what's his real name.

ii The teacher asked what his real name was.

d 'I saw a red car nearby,' a witness reported. (direct)

i The witness reported seeing a red car nearby.

ii The witness reported that he sees a red car nearby.

UNIT FIFTEEN

Mist and fog

Focus

Sentence fragments; run-on sentences

Grammar in use

Text A

Losing his way. Fog all around. The boy shivered. He could no longer see his hand in front of his face. **If he tripped.** If he just kept walking he might walk over a cliff. Or into a tree. He was lost and he knew it. **Being a sensible boy.** He stood still and listened for something that might tell him where he was. **Nothing at all.**

Text B

He had lost his way. There was fog all around him. The boy shivered. He could no longer see his hand in front of his face. **If he tripped he could slip into a gully.** If he just kept walking he might walk over a cliff or into a tree. He was lost and he knew it. Being a sensible boy he stood still and listened for something that might tell him where he was. He heard nothing at all.

Text B is much easier to follow than Text A. Text A contains many groups of words that are punctuated as sentences but make no sense on their own. These 'part-sentences' are called **sentence fragments**.

- **Losing his way. Being a sensible boy.** (Who was losing his way and who was a sensible boy?) These fragments have **no subject** and **no complete verb**.
- **Fog all around.** (Fog is all around what?) This fragment has **no verb** and **no object**.
- **If he tripped.** (What would happen?) This fragment is a **dependent clause** with no meaning unless a main clause is added, as in: **If he tripped** *he could slip into a gully.*
- We sometimes use fragments in speech and informal writing such as emails and stories, but **only if the context allows the reader to understand the meaning**. However, fragments have no place in formal writing such as essays and reports; for example, *Where's the torch?* **In the desk by the window**. (fragment in informal speech) *Jasmine found the torch in the desk by the door.* (complete sentence in formal writing)
- In Text A, the fragments **Fog all around** and **Nothing at all** are acceptable because **we know what is meant**, but the other fragments are not—they are too incomplete.

Common fragment errors are

- ***ing* clauses**; for example, *Being very cold/Having no coat on/Knowing he needed help.*
- **prepositional phrases**; for example, *Near the edge/Near the summit.*
- clauses beginning with ***which*** or ***who***; for example, *Which he wanted/Whoever heard his call.*
- clauses beginning with **conjunctions**; for example, *Until the fog cleared/Before the sun came out.*

Boost your grammar skills

1 Write *S* for **sentence** or *F* for **fragment** beside each of these.

- **a** Going away. ______
- **b** Found under a rock. ______
- **c** Having been lost. ______
- **d** Which hid the view. ______
- **e** The fog was dense. ______
- **f** She was confused. ______
- **g** Always on my mind. ______
- **h** Abandoned in the forest and beset by fear. ______
- **i** After eating a meal. ______
- **j** Being afraid, he wished was not alone. ______

2 Make complete sentences by adding one of these to each **fragment**. Add full stops and commas.

turned it gold	was a blanket of fog
the mist was beginning to lift	slowed to a crawl in the fog
paddle silently in the mist	

- **a** Ducks on the river ______________________________
- **b** Traffic already heavy ______________________________
- **c** Shafts of sunlight streaming through the mist ______________________________
- **d** Settled over the surface of the reservoir ______________________________
- **e** It being already an hour after sunrise ______________________________

3 Circle one word that must be deleted in each **fragment** to make a complete sentence.

- **a** When I heard you.
- **b** As the lamp light flamed.
- **c** While I put on a coat and hat.
- **d** Since the moon rose in a halo of frost.
- **e** Unless you tell her.
- **f** Until the mist vapours dissipated.
- **g** If he should go out.
- **h** Before the evening fog closed in.
- **i** Because kettle steam burns.
- **j** Whether he should go skiing.

4 Circle the correct alternative.

- **a** **i** Craig, having a cold and being absent from training.
  - **ii** Craig, having a cold, was absent from training.

b **i** Generally delayed by sea fog, the ferry is on time today.

ii Generally delayed by sea fog, the ferry being on time today.

c **i** Being a cold damp country. Houses in England often have problems with rising damp.

ii Houses in England, a cold damp country, often have problems with rising damp.

d **i** She stood to one side thinking. Drinking a hot chocolate.

ii She stood to one side thinking and drinking a hot chocolate.

e **i** To create an eerie atmosphere, use a fog machine.

ii To create an eerie atmosphere using a fog machine.

5 Underline the **fragments** in this text.

> Contrary to popular belief. Mist and fog are not the same natural phenomena. While mist rises from the ground. Fog descends to the ground from the atmosphere. The expressions 'fog settling' and 'mist rising'.

6 Rewrite these short texts without any **fragments**. There is more than one way to do this. You may need to add extra words and change words.

a The waratah flourishes best in a cold climate. Thriving in deep wet mountain valleys.

____

____

b Callum looked out. Unknown figure in the mist. Striding purposefully towards the house.

____

____

c Being confused. Steam filled the bathroom. I walked into the door and broke my nose.

____

____

d We all tried to remain hopeful. Which was difficult in the circumstances.

____

____

e Melting on the windows. Frost turned into rivulets down the glass. Puddles on the sill.

____

____

7 In which texts are the **fragments** suited to the context?

a Dear John, having a great time. Wish you were here. Leo.

b Carrying an oxygen tank. The climbers avoided the risk of altitude.

c Whiteout occurs in an Antarctic blizzard. Snow in the air and snow all around.

d We turned the bend and there it was at last. Our little hut. Snug and warm and waiting.

Punctuation in use

Text A

Sea fog over the harbour renders everything invisible you cannot see the bridge the ferries or the early morning fishermen rocking at anchor ship foghorns in the gloom announce the presence of incoming container vessels they need tugboats to pilot them into the harbour terminal.

Text B

Sea fog over the harbour renders everything invisible. You cannot see the bridge, the ferries or the early morning fishermen rocking at anchor. Ship foghorns in the gloom announce the presence of incoming container vessels that need tugboats to pilot them into the harbour terminal.

About punctuation

Text B is easier to read than Text A. The writer uses full stops to separate one idea from another into meaningful sentences. Text A runs all the sentences together. We call two or more sentences run together like this **run-ons**.

A run-on occurs

- when two or more sentences are **run together without full stops** or conjunctions to join them as in Text A.
- when two or more sentences are **run together with commas** instead of full stops or conjunctions; for example, *The lighthouse beam shone through the fog, the sailors cried out in relief.* (run-on)/*The lighthouse beam shone through the fog. The sailors cried out in relief.* (two sentences)/*The lighthouse beam shone through the fog and the sailors cried out in relief.* (one sentence joined by a conjunction).

Boost your punctuation skills

1 Write *S* for **sentence** and *R* for **run-on**.

a On foggy nights the call of the tawny frogmouth sounds lonely. ______

b Mrs Halim was burned by steam her kettle had no lid on when she picked it up. ______

c Jockeys must sweat off excess weight before a race they sit in saunas for hours. ______

d The barn owl's face mask gathers light it so it can see even on a moonless night. ______

e Carley batted first she hit a six the ball disappeared into the wintry mist fielders did not know where to look. ______

2 Rewrite these **run-ons** as two or three sentences each. There is more than one way to do this. You may need to add conjunctions to some.

a Ghost stories frighten me they all feature dark nights and strange noises I get totally spooked.

____

____

b Where are you I can't see you I can't see anything at all

c The fog thinned the sun rose high in the sky the seals decided to sun themselves on ice floes.

d The mountain was silent everything was white suddenly they heard a great roar an avalanche swept past the shaken skiers.

e Lighthouses in Bass Strait have saved many ships and their crews great storms wrack the Strait fog regularly this makes rocks and small islands invisible

3 These **run-ons** have used commas incorrectly. Rewrite them using conjunctions and correct punctuation. You may end up with more than one sentence.

a The fog descended without warning, it covered the land like a blanket, he did not know where he was.

b Pilots engage the auto pilot, they fly through thick banks of clouds, visibility is non-existent.

c The Lady of the Lake rose out of the water through the trailing mists of the night, Arthur caught sight of a magnificent sword in her hand.

UNIT SIXTEEN

Mixed messages

Focus

Ambiguous sentences; apostrophe review

Grammar in use

These sentences all make sense so what is the problem?

1. 'Michael, will you give me a **ring** on Friday night?' his girlfriend asked.
2. Lisa gave her friend **her** books.
3. The boy confessed that he had taken the money **yesterday**.
4. We are having the Smiths **for** dinner on Sunday.
5. The man was arrested before any damage was done **by police**.
6. I know a lady with a cat **who has fleas**.
7. **After being roasted on one side**, she turned the chicken over.

- The problem with the sentences above is that they have more than one meaning. They are **ambiguous**. Each sentence demonstrates one kind of ambiguity.
  - In **1** is the ring a telephone call or a friendship ring? The problem here is that the word **ring** is ambiguous. An unambiguous sentence would say: *Michael, will you phone me ...?* or *Michael, will you give me a friendship ring ...?*
  - In **2** whose books were given, Lisa's books or the friend's? It is not clear to whom the pronoun **her** relates. An unambiguous sentence would say: *Lisa gave her friend's books to* **her** or *Lisa gave her books to* **her** *friend on loan.*
  - In **3** did the boy confess yesterday or take the money yesterday? Misplaced adverbs cause ambiguity. An unambiguous sentence would say: *The boy* **confessed yesterday** *that he had taken the money.* or *The boy* **confessed that yesterday** *he had taken the money.*
  - In **4** are we going to eat the Smiths? The incorrect preposition **for** has caused this ambiguity. An unambiguous sentence would say: *We are having the Smiths* **to** *dinner on Sunday.*
  - In **5** is it the man or the police who might do the damage? This ambiguity is caused by the misplacement of the phrase **by police**. An unambiguous sentence would say: *The man was arrested* **by police** *before any damage was done.*
  - In **6** who has the fleas, the lady or the cat? Here the problem is the dependent clause **who has fleas**. An unambiguous sentence would say: *I know a lady* **whose cat has fleas**.
  - In **7** who was roasted on all sides, the woman or the chicken? Here the problem is the placement of the clause **After being roasted on one side** next to the pronoun *she*. One way to make it unambiguous is to say: **After she roasted the chicken on one side**, *she turned it over.*

Boost your grammar skills

1 Write the **two possible meanings** of each of these sentences by adding words in the spaces. There is more than one possible answer.

a The miner cut into a vein.

i The miner cut into a ____________________.

ii The miner cut into a ____________________.

b Mr Gill is the French teacher.

i Mr Gill is ____________________.

ii Mr Gill is ____________________.

c The new mouse is dead.

i The new ____________________.

ii The new ____________________.

2 Rewrite these headlines and advertisements so that **only one meaning** is possible (the most likely meaning).

For example: Cat Caught by Man Spitting and Hissing
Man Catches Spitting Hissing Cat

a Stolen Jewellery Found by Statue

____

b Dog Attacks Man With Wooden Leg

____

c Brothers Reunited after Twenty Years in Library

____

d Snake Bites Child with Bare Feet

____

e Red Tape holds up New Bridge

____

3 Write *A* for **ambiguous** statements and *C* for **clear** statements.

a If your baby bird cannot swallow seed, grind it into mash with water. ______

b He gave his friend cat food for his new tabby cat. ______

c Leaping out of the sea, the boat was swamped by a whale. ______

d Unless you eat well you will grow thin and ill. ______

e Snakes can be a danger to careless walkers. ______

f That man was struck by a lady wielding an umbrella. ______

g The teacher said on Monday he would set an exam. ______

4 One sentence in each pair is completely clear (**unambiguous**). Tick (✔) that sentence.

a **i** Swimming underwater the octopus kept one black eye on us. ______

ii The octopus kept one black eye on us as we swam underwater. ______

b **i** Woken suddenly from his nap, Jasper was bitten on the foot by a brown snake. ______

ii A brown snake, woken suddenly from his nap, bit Jasper on the foot. ______

c **i** I want the cream cakes in that window. ______

ii I want the cakes in that window with cream. ______

d **i** Wandering through the bush vines scratched us with their thorns. ______

ii Vines scratched us with their thorns as we wandered through the bush. ______

e **i** Michael told Jai that his jeans were ripped. ______

ii 'Jai, your jeans are ripped,' said Michael. ______

5 Rewrite these so that there is **only one possible meaning**. You may need to add words as well as change them.

a Mrs Turner discussed her son's problems with his teachers.

____

____

b We saw the man with Mark's binoculars.

____

____

c Her children make lovely chocolate crackles.

____

____

d I'll hold the nail and when I nod my head, hit it with the hammer.

____

____

e He was tall with a craggy face from the bank.

____

____

f I saw a man on a bike with muttonchop whiskers.

____

____

g When only four Fergus' grandfather took him to an AFL match.

____

____

Punctuation in use

Text A

Last week my brother and I had our first **kayaking lessons'** at the **Sandhill whitewater rafting Centre**. Mostly it was boys who turned up but there were about **eight girl's** too. My brother Leo had to go **in the girls group** so he wasnt happy at first, but he ended up having a great time. Our instructor was Jose from **south America**. Hes over here in Sydney for training. I cant wait for **next weeks lesson**. Its such great fun. Im hoping that I will advance quickly and get into a higher group soon.

Text B

Last week my brother and I had our first **kayaking lessons** at the **Sandhill Whitewater Rafting Centre**. Mostly it was boys who turned up but there were about **eight girls** too. My brother Leo had to go **in the girls' group** so he wasn't happy at first, but he ended up having a great time. Our instructor was Jose from **South America**. He's over here in Sydney for training. I can't wait for **next week's lesson**. It's such great fun. I'm hoping that I will advance quickly and get into a higher group soon.

About punctuation

Text A is missing some capital letters and apostrophes, and has used some apostrophes incorrectly. Text B is correct.

- Remember: **proper nouns begin with capital letters** and must be used for all words in the name or title; for example, *Sandhill **w**hitewater **r**afting **C**entre* (✗)/*Sandhill **W**hitewater **R**afting **C**entre* (✓)/*south **A**merica* (incorrect), ***S**outh **A**merica* (✓).
- **Apostrophes of possession** are used to show that someone owns something else; for example, *the girl**s** group, next week**s** lesson* (✗)/*the girl**s'** group, next week**'s** lesson* (✓).
- Apostrophes are **NOT** needed simply to show plural; for example, *kayaking lesson**s'**, eight girl**'s*** (✗)/*kayaking lesson**s**, eight girl**s*** (✓).
- If you need to revise all the rules for adding the apostrophe of possession, look back at Chapter 11.
- **Apostrophes of contraction** are used to show that letters are missing in a word; for example, *wasnt, hes, cant, its, Im* (✗)/*wasn't, he's (he is), can't, it's, I'm* (✓).
- If you need to revise all the rules for adding the apostrophe of contraction, look back at Chapter 9.
- Note: beware of confusion with ***it's*** (*it is*) and ***its*** (possessive pronoun meaning 'belonging to it'). If you can't replace *it's* with *it is* in the sentence, then you need *its*.

Boost your punctuation skills

1 Revise **capital letters** and **end punctuation** by correcting these sentences.

a australian teams usually do well in international rowing

b where is the local skateboard park

c surfing lessons are held every sunday at west avalon surf club

d is new zealand beating australia in the world cup

e Hey we beat the western redbacks

2 Circle the alternative that uses the **apostrophe of possession** correctly.

a A (ship's/ships') kitchen is called a galley.

b The (men's/mens) cabins were towards the stern of the ship.

c (Sailors'/sailor's) beds are called bunks or hammocks.

d The (women's/womens) team were victorious.

e The (boy's/boys') kayak overturned in the wash from a launch and they went under.

f The (competitors/competitors') all finished their races with good times.

3 Put a cross (✗) next to those below which use the **apostrophe** incorrectly or which are missing an apostrophe. Then write the words correctly.

a New Potatoes' Today ______

b Todays Special—Minestrone soup ______

c Latest styles' here today ______

d Footwear Specialists' ______

e Children's haircuts $5 only! ______

f Chicken and Fries to go! ______

g All Your Petcare Need's Here ______

h Neptunes' Haven ______

Corrections:

____

____

____

____

____

____

4 Tick (✓) the correct sentence.

a i I haven't seen you here before. ______

ii I have'nt seen you here before. ______

b i We shouldn't swim after dark. ______

ii We should'nt swim after dark. ______

c i Their my oranges. ______

ii They're my oranges. ______

d i Its' not compulsory to attend. ______

ii It's not compulsory to attend. ______

e i The dog shook its head. ______

ii The dog shook it's head. ______

f i We're losing. ______

ii Where losing. ______

g i Who's playing today? ______

ii Whose playing today? ______

h i Their were three boats. ______

ii There were three boats. ______

5 Strike out any incorrect **punctuation** and add any missing punctuation in the text below.

> know what you want to say. make sure its logical then write it carefully paying attention to grammar and using all necessary punctuation. If you do this youre going to be a good writer you may even become a great writer and figure in the lists' of the top bestsellers of our age

6 Tick (✔) the correct sentences and cross (✘) the incorrect ones.

a I think these books are theirs! ______

b They're too late for the bus, they've missed the game. ______

c The scissor's blades are blunt. ______

d I'm prepared for wet weather but your'e not. ______

e Tom couldnt' open the window. ______

7 Write an appropriate **abbreviated word** in each space.

a Hamid ______________ be able to play because he has the 'flu.

b If the girls swim there ______________ going to be stung by blue bottles.

c The truck rolled over and ______________ going to take some time to be moved.

d Although you ______________ brought your gear, you can still play.

e If you ______________ there you can't comment.

8 Write *it's* or *its* in the spaces as appropriate.

a ______________ raining in Queensland. All ______________ rivers are in flood. All ______________ residents are wet and ______________ only going to get worse.

b 'Is it true that snakes can swim?' Tom asked as he looked out at the floodwaters. 'Yes ______________ true, all right. There's a snake right there and ______________ swimming easily. I don't think ______________ lost ______________ cool at all,' Mike answered.

Revision Test 4

Grammar

Shade one circle to show the correct answer.

1 Which sentence is the most certain?

- ◯ I might just finish this by tonight.
- ◯ I could finish this by tonight.
- ◯ Perhaps I will finish this by tonight.
- ◯ I will finish this by tonight.

2 Which sentence indicates that the speaker is not certain?

- ◯ I might go sailing if the sea is not too choppy.
- ◯ I will go sailing if the sea is not too choppy.
- ◯ I must go sailing if the sea is not too choppy.

3 Which word completes this sentence with certainty?

All students ________________ be considerate of others.

- ◯ may
- ◯ might
- ◯ must
- ◯ could

4 Which sentence shows the speaker is not sure?

- ◯ I'm going to Indonesia next year.
- ◯ I will go to Indonesia next year.
- ◯ I may go to Indonesia next year.
- ◯ I won't go to Indonesia next year.

5 Which sentence is written in the active voice?

- ◯ The policeman chased the thief.
- ◯ The thief was chased by the policeman.

6 Which sentence is written in the passive voice?

- ◯ Bulldozers were demolishing the house at number 5.
- ◯ Bulldozers demolished the old house at number 5.
- ◯ The house at number 5 was demolished by bulldozers.

7 Which words are missing from this sentence?

We ________________ to accept the apology.

- ◯ persuaded
- ◯ were persuading
- ◯ were persuaded

8 This sentence is written in the active voice:

We spent most of our time swimming.

Which of the sentences below is the passive voice form of the sentence?

- ◯ We are spending most of our time swimming.
- ◯ Most of our time was spent swimming.
- ◯ Most of the time we were swimming.

In questions 9–11, which one is a sentence?

9
- ◯ A chill wind.
- ◯ A chill wind through the open door.
- ◯ A chill wind gusted through the open door.
- ◯ A chill wind through the open door in the far wall.

10
- ◯ Whales leaping high out of the water.
- ◯ Southern right whales leaping out of the water.
- ◯ Southern right whales leaping out of the water delighted tourists.

11
- ◯ Being frightened out of his wits
- ◯ Michael, being frightened out of his wits, hid behind the steel door.
- ◯ Michael being frightened out of his wits behind the steel door.

In questions 12–13, which one is **not** a sentence?

12
- ◯ Over there beyond the trees you can see a mob of kangaroos.
- ◯ A mob of kangaroos is grazing over there beyond the trees.
- ◯ Kangaroos grazing over there beyond the trees.

13
- ◯ Seals sunning themselves on the rocks below the cliff.
- ◯ Seals were sunning themselves.
- ◯ Seals were sunning themselves on the rocks.
- ◯ Seals are sunning themselves.

In questions 14–16, which one is ambiguous (not clear)?

14
- ◯ Experts say bus passengers should be belted.
- ◯ Experts say passengers should be belted to their seats.
- ◯ Experts say bus passengers should wear seat belts.

15
- ◯ Kyra told Bonnie that Bonnie owed her a dollar.
- ◯ Kyra told Bonnie she owed her a dollar.
- ◯ Kyra told Bonnie, "You owe me a dollar."

16
- ◯ If your sink tap is leaking, replace it immediately.
- ◯ Replace a leaking sink tap immediately.
- ◯ If your sink has a leaking tap, replace it immediately.

17 Which words are missing from this sentence?

The door ____________________ by the shopkeeper.

- ◯ locked
- ◯ was locking
- ◯ had been locked
- ◯ will be locking

Punctuation

1 Which sentence is correctly punctuated?

- ◯ My neighbour the one who's the skydiver had a car accident yesterday.
- ◯ My neighbour (the one who's the skydiver) had a car accident yesterday.
- ◯ My neighbour 'the one who's the skydiver' had a car accident yesterday.

2 Brackets have been left out of this sentence. Where should they go?

Ornithology ◯ the ◯ study of birds ◯ is pursued today ◯ by scientific methods.

3 Which sentence uses indirect speech?

- ◯ 'Where has Mia been?' asked Duncan.
- ◯ Duncan asked where Mia had been.

In questions 4–7, which sentence is correctly punctuated?

4
- ◯ We're having spinach pie for lunch—I hate spinach pie—with ice-cream for sweets.
- ◯ We're having spinach pie for lunch, I hate spinach pie, with ice-cream for sweets.
- ◯ We're having spinach pie for lunch—I hate spinach pie with ice-cream for sweets.

5
- ◯ He asked why the fence had been cut?
- ◯ He asked why the fence had been cut.

6
- ◯ 'My pigeon he said has flown two hundred miles and back.'
- ◯ 'My pigeon he said' has flown two hundred miles and back.
- ◯ 'My pigeon,' he said has flown two hundred miles and back.
- ◯ 'My pigeon,' he said 'has flown two hundred miles and back.'

7
- ◯ Elise has red hair she plays the violin and she's very talented.
- ◯ Elise has red hair and she plays violin she's very talented.
- ◯ Elise has red hair she plays the violin she's very talented.
- ◯ Elise has red hair. She plays the violin. She's very talented.

8 Where should the six missing full stops be placed?

We went to the Entertainment Centre ◯ for the Drifters concert ◯ it was an amazing night ◯ everyone was singing along ◯ the crowd was so thick ◯ we could hardly move ◯ we all got very hot ◯ under the blazing lights ◯ some people fainted ◯

In questions 9–13, which sentence is correct?

9
- ◯ Are you wearing you're hat?
- ◯ Are you wearing your hat?

10 ◯ Those tickets are theirs.
◯ Those tickets are theirs'.
◯ Those tickets are their's.

11 ◯ That house has lost its roof.
◯ That house has lost it's roof.

12 ◯ The tree lost it's leaves
◯ The tree lost its' leaves.
◯ The tree lost its leaves.
◯ The tree lost their leaves

13 ◯ Tomatos for sale
◯ Tomatoes for sale.
◯ Tomatoe's for sale.
◯ Tomatoes' for sale.

14 Which is the correct alternative?

Summer is fun. (Its/it's) the season when we can swim every day.

◯ It's ◯ Its

In questions 15–16, which sentence is correctly punctuated?

15 ◯ Mrs Eddy asked for every girls science book.
◯ Mrs Eddy asked for every girl's science book.
◯ Mrs Eddy asked for every girls' science book.

16 ◯ The puppie's tails all wagged in unison.
◯ The puppies' tails' all wagged in unison.
◯ The puppies' tails all wagged in unison.
◯ The puppies' tail's all wagged in unison.

17 An apostrophe has been left out of this sentence. Where should it go?

◯ ◯ ◯

It ↓ is everyone ↓ s responsibility to drive safely on road ↓ s and freeway.

Answers

UNIT 1 A round blue world

Grammar pages 2–3

1 Lakes are large bodies of water surrounded by land. In Australia, Lake Eyre is a dry salt lake that fills with runoff from heavy rains in Queensland. In Africa, Lake Victoria is a huge deep lake that supports fish, waterbirds, animals and people. The White Nile flows from this lake, joins the Blue Nile from Ethiopia, and so becomes the mighty Nile that reaches the Mediterranean Sea.

2 **a** Eyre **b** Amazon **c** Mexico **d** French **e** Irishman **f** Kosciusko **g** Moscow **h** Sahara

3 Proper nouns: Krakatoa, Indonesia

Collective nouns: series, flocks, herds

Abstract nouns: fear, fright, confusion

4 In ancient times (common) **sailors** went to sea in (abstract) **fear** and (abstract) **trepidation**. They believed the (concrete) **world** was flat like a (concrete) **table** and that they would fall off its (concrete) **edge** if they travelled too far into unknown waters. In the sixteenth century Portuguese seamen, Ferdinand Magellan and (proper) **Juan Sebastian Delcano** sailed right around the world proving that it is a (concrete) **globe**, not a table.

5 **a** proper **b** proper **c** concrete **d** abstract **e** collective **f** proper **g** concrete **h** abstract **i** proper

6 **b** mountain ✗ Africa ✗ Kilimanjaro ✓

c earthquakes ✓ earthquakes ✗

d water ✓ craters ✓ beauty ✓ colours ✗

7 **a** **Antarctica** is a huge frozen landmass at the southern tip of the world.

b Penguins, walrus and **seals**/**albatross**/**seabirds** live in the Southern Ocean.

c Tasmania was part of the **continent**/**mainland** of Australia until the sea flooded Bass Strait.

d The **fear** of being upturned by a whale disturbed the sleep of many an old-time sailor.

e At dusk a **flock** of ibis headed west into the sunset.

Punctuation pages 4–5

1 **a** The Rhine flows from Switzerland through France, Germany, Belgium and The Netherlands.

b Container ships, bulk ore carriers, oil tankers and ocean liners travel the high seas.

c The Paroo, Warrego, Namoi, Bogan, Macquarie and Castlereagh rivers all flow into the Darling River.

d Travelling south along the Nile you pass through the countries of Egypt, North Sudan, South Sudan and Uganda.

e Lake Baikal, the Caspian Sea, the Aral Sea and the Black Sea are all large inland stretches of water in Europe and Asia.

f Freight barges, eel boats, tourist ships and small rowing boats ply the waters of the Rhine.

g Ships on the Great Lakes of North America carry household goods, wheat, timber, oil and machinery between cities.

When we travelled to Lake Eyre in South Australia, we camped beside the water. We were woken the next morning by a great noise. The lake was covered with thousands of birds. There were pelicans, ibis, herons, spoonbills and every kind of waterbird imaginable. My father was especially happy because he saw a banded stilt. My sister spied a freckled duck so she was happy too. On the long trip home we crossed over the **N**orthern Territory, **Q**ueensland and **N**ew **S**outh **W**ales borders.

3 The waters, ✗ of the Indian Ocean, ✗ wash the coasts of Australia, Indonesia, Thailand, India, Saudi Arabia, ✗ and all the countries, ✗ of Africa's east coast. It also surrounds islands, ✗ like the Maldives, Sri Lanka, ✗ and Madagascar.

4 **b** Some of the rivers that flow into the Darling River are the Paroo, Warrego, Namoi, Bogan, Macquarie and Castlereagh rivers.

c Four large inland seas are Lake Baikal, the Caspian Sea, the Black Sea and the Aral seas.

d Australian waterbirds include pelicans, ibis, herons, spoonbills, freckled ducks and banded stilts.

e Some countries are islands, including Australia, Greenland, Japan and Indonesia.

5 **a** The warm current off the coast of **A**ustralia brings whales**,** penguins and seals up to feed.

b The **G**reat **B**arrier **R**eef is home to corals**,** eels**,** rays**,** shellfish**,** sharks and myriads of fish.

c The **T**odd **R**iver in **A**lice **S**prings is usually dry.

d Lake **J**indabyne is a man-made lake that is home to trout**,** redfin**,** eels and cod.

e Passage across a river can be gained via stepping stones**,** a ford**,** a causeway**,** a fallen log**,** a flying fox or a bridge.

f Caves beneath the ground are networks of narrow passageways**,** chambers of various sizes and sudden drops into the darkness.

UNIT 2 Living together

Grammar pages 6–8

1 From the far end of the pool came a scream followed by a splash. Taha didn't hesitate. He plunged straight in and headed for the deep end, his arms churning the water into froth. A little redheaded girl was struggling in the water. She stayed under longer each time she sank. The crowd roared its approval as Taha reached her and then, by rolling over onto his back, towed her to the wall of the pool and safety.

2 Joe, Kamal and the boys went down to the creek. Joe told them there were plenty of yellowbelly to be caught. Kamal threw in a line and soon he felt something snatch at it. Scott yelled that he could see something on the end of Kamal's line. The line raced from the rod so fast they had to hold the rod steady as Kamal slowly reeled in the line. With a great spray of water an old man eel flipped onto the bank. It was all of two metres in length.

3 **a** her, her, it

b him, his, them, him

c They, They

4 **b** theirs **c** hers **d** ours

e yours

5 Her, she, They, their

6 The boys were all playing tag on the basketball court. Peter tripped over and broke **his** arm. Eddie and **his** mate took Peter up to the sick bay. Jemal carried **his** bag because Peter was too hurt to carry **it**.

7 **We** all agreed to meet at eleven o'clock. **We** were to bring a picnic lunch, our towels and **our** suncream. **We** should all bring **our** mozzie repellent too. It was a great summer for all of **us**. Sun, surf, sand, beach cricket and friendship—what more could any of **us** want?

8 **a** ✓ **b** ✗ **c** ✓ **d** ✓ **e** ✓

Punctuation pages 9–10

1 **a** Charlie and Dave**,** fishing mates for years**,** are out on Jervis Bay looking for bream.

b May I sit with you in the library**,** Aziza?

c Omar's uncle**,** a doctor**,** was born in Cairo in Egypt.

d Uncle David**,** Mum's brother**,** is coming to visit at the weekend.

e Shut the window**,** Michael. It's very windy**,** don't you think?

2 Mrs Zanetti, ✗ and Mrs Markson, next door, ✗ neighbours, share the produce of their gardens. Zannetti hens, ✗ keep the Markson family in eggs and Markson tomatoes help to make the rich Zanetti tomato sauce. It's great for neighbours, ✗ to share the things they grow, I reckon.

3 Thirteen is really grown up, I think. My friends Amy, Alice and Joy agree. Do Mum and Dad think so too, I wonder? They let us go ten pin bowling by ourselves this afternoon. I asked Mum later if she thought I was grown up now. She said I was getting there. Parents, mothers in particular, really are annoying sometimes, aren't they? They never give you a straight answer.

4
- **a** Greg, Leo, Andy and Louis play squash together every Friday.
- **b** Have you lost your compass again, Craig? You must have a hole in your backpack, I think.
- **c** Netball, basketball, soccer, tennis and squash are the winter sport options.
- **d** The Magpies, the Under-14s, were named Best and Fairest in the Interschool competition.
- **e** Blue, Sarg, Crow and Tadpole were our nicknames in primary school.
- **f** Marie, will you play chess with me at lunchtime?

5 Safi's words are correctly punctuated.

6 It's not a comet, a comb, a candle or a cradle;
it's not even a camel or a crystal candelabra.
It looks more like a tadpole, I think,
and has a tail like a cat but
a comma's not furred and certainly can't swim—
of that we are sure, dear Harry, my friend—
so we'll go with an ink spin that
splotted a dot, and dribbled a squiggle
and that's the lot—for a comma.

UNIT 3

All creatures great and small

Grammar pages 12–13

1
- **a** gorilla beat
- **b** goats were leaping
- **c** jaguars hunt
- **d** meerkat fled
- **e** snake slid

2 **a** is **b** are **c** are **d** is **e** were

3 **a** would **b** will **c** has **d** have **e** have **f** do

4
- **a** sounds
- **b** feels, is
- **c** stay
- **d** look, are
- **e** looks

5

Present	Simple past	Future	Continuous present	Continuous past
hiss	hissed	will hiss	is hissing	was hissing
stalk	**stalked**	**will stalk**	is stalking	**was stalking**
hibernates	hibernated	will hibernate	**is hibernating**	**was hibernating**
prey	**preyed**	**will prey**	**is preying**	**was preying**
howl	**howled**	**will howl**	is howling	**was howling**

6
- **b** is imitating
- **c** was sunning
- **d** were flitting
- **e** is cruising

7 Patch was a tiny ball of fluff when a cyclist found him in the dust by the roadside. The little ringtail was so small the cyclist buttoned him into his shirt pocket and ferried him to a wildlife carer who was happy to care for the little orphan. She made him a little nest and fed him native flowers and fruit till he grew into handsome adult. Then she returned him to the Australian bush.

8 Last night I heard a loud huff and hiss outside my window. I **looked** out and there **was** a large brushtail possum sitting on a branch staring at me. He **had** bright black eyes. His little button nose was pink and he **was**

holding one of Mum's roses in paws that looked just like little dark hands. He was very handsome but when he hissed loudly at another possum I **thought** he **sounded** as if he could be quite cross.

Punctuation pages 14–15

1

a Unfortunately**,** we have not seen a night parrot for several decades in Australia.

b Look**,** there's a microbat flying past the old kurrajong tree.

c It's raining. Nevertheless**,** the seagulls are still scavenging on the beach.

d South America's boa constrictor can**,** in fact**,** crush and swallow a full-grown pig.

e Sadly**,** the bandicoots of Sydney are now found only in two small areas.

f Unbelievably**,** lyrebirds can mimic both a chainsaw and a fire siren.

g Butterflies**,** as a general rule**,** sleep with wings upright while moths sleep with folded wings.

2

a Quickly**,** close the gate before the cattle get out.

b Look**,** that's an orb spider building its three-dimensional web.

c Gosh**,** see this! The peacock's showing off his fan feathers.

d Hey**,** look at this! The bees are swarming.

e Heavens above**,** what will that dolphin do next?

3

a Hopefully**,** there will be no mouse plague, ✗ this summer.

b The cane, ✗ toad**,** unhappily**,** has been a disaster, ✗ for Australian wildlife.

c Saltwater crocodiles, in fact, have remained, ✗ almost unchanged, ✗ since the age of the dinosaurs.

d Feral cats**,** unexpectedly**,** go back to their wild size as well as their wild habits.

e Tragically**,** New Zealand's moa was hunted, ✗ to extinction, ✗ in the nineteenth century.

4 b ✗ d ✗ e ✗

5 Meerkats**,** like penguins**,** live in colonies. They share multiple burrows and**,** unusually**,** take turns in looking after their young. Routinely**,** they set one meerkat to watch for danger**,** some to clean the burrows and others to hunt for food. Nevertheless**,** every meerkat stays on the alert for danger. Babysitters carefully mind the colony's young and keep a wary eye out for danger.

6 a ✗ b ✓ c ✓ d ✗

UNIT 4 How it all works

Grammar pages 17–18

1

a Ocean tides [rise] and [fall] according to the moon's gravitational pull.

b Weightlessness in space [can waste] an astronaut's muscles.

c Astronauts [were repairing] a loose surface tile when they [dropped] a spanner into space.

d Those space engineers [are wearing] very heavy boots so they don't [float] away.

e Space junk often [becomes] a hazard for spacecraft.

2

b A mountain spring

c A dust storm

d Glowing lava flows

e The tremors

3

a The mountains catch rainfall from the sea.

b Floods enrich the land.

c Rivers fill South Australia's Lake Eyre.

d Most earthquakes occur on fault lines.

4

a chills b flood c cause
d bury e bring

5

a C b S c S
d C e C

6

a The Earth revolves around the sun **and** at the same time it revolves on its own axis.

b Solar power is safe **but** some places do not have enough sunshine for solar energy.

c The wind is picking up **so** it must be going to rain.

d We must take shelter **or** the storm will overtake us.

e Don't stand under trees in a storm **or** lightning might strike you.

f We live every day with the sun right above us **but** most of us know very little about it.

7 **a** ✗ **b** ✗ **e** ✗

8 Watching the sky. A strange green light. A scurry of leaves.

Punctuation pages 19–20

1
- **a** The United Nations
- **b** The International Red Cross
- **c** The World Wildlife Fund
- **d** Taronga Park Zoo
- **e** Keep Australia Beautiful
- **f** Friends of the Earth

2
- **a** *The Sorcerer's Apprentice*
- **b** *The Fellowship of the Ring*
- **c** *A Midsummer Night's Dream*
- **d** *The Obernewtyn Chronicles*
- **e** *Pride and Prejudice*
- **f** *Harry Potter and the Deathly Hallows*

3
- **a** Chernobyl, Fukushima
- **b** Urumchi, China
- **c** The International Space Station, Earth
- **d** Iron, Kimberley, Western
- **e** The Three Gorges Dam, China

4
- **a** Christmas, December, Jesus
- **b** Diwali, Hindu, Festival of Lights
- **c** Hanukkah, Jewish, Festival of Lights
- **d** Eid il Fitr, Muslim, Ramadan
- **e** The, Buddhism, Tripitaka

5 **T**hirty days hath **S**eptember,
April, **J**une and **N**ovember.
All the rest have thirty-one
save **F**ebruary alone
which has twenty-eight days clear
and twenty-nine each leap
year.

6
- **a** **R**everend Charles Turner
- **b** **H**is **R**oyal Highness **K**ing **J**igme **W**anchuk of **B**hutan
- **c** **G**overnor **G**eneral of **A**ustralia
- **d** Captain **F**ogarty **F**egan of **HMAS** **J**ervis **B**ay
- **e** **E**mperor **N**apoleon of France
- **f** Ben Chifley, **P**rime **M**inister of **A**ustralia

7 **S**ailing ship captains knew to sail **s**outh from the **E**quator until they reached the **G**reat **S**outhern **O**cean. **H**ere they could catch the trade winds that would carry them east until they reached the **P**acific **O**cean. **T**he only problem was sailing through the stormy **B**ass **S**trait between the mainland of Australia and **T**asmania. Tragically, many **s**hips have perished in those treacherous **s**eas.

Revision Test 1

Grammar pages 21–23

1 seal, shark, fish, crab, whale

2 stable

3 Sydney

4 Tasmania

5 chair

6 tables

7 anxiety

8 picture

9 concrete noun

10 flock

11 herd, fleet, team, crew

12 buffaloes

13 we

14 her

15 she

16 her

17 theirs

18 swim, investigate, descend, dive

19 is

20 will carry

21 are

22 The choir sang in four-part harmony yesterday.

23 All the students are on holidays.

24 Riley and Sam are going skiing this weekend.

25 Maria and her friends enjoy bird watching in the National Park.

Punctuation

pages 24–25

1 rice,

2 speaking,

3 Wow, see how red Mars looks tonight.

4 The campers each carried a tent, water, food and a hat.

5 Samantha, will you show Isaac where the library is, please.

6 The crocodile, native to north Australia, is considered a living dinosaur.

7 He piled grass and twigs, lit a match and blew hard to encourage a flame.

8 Lisa goes to netball on Saturdays unless, of course, it is raining.

9 New Zealand's Mount Tarawera volcano exploded in 1886.

10 Koalas and wombats are first cousins.

11 Joern Utzon, a Danish architect, designed the Sydney Opera House.

12 The Tropic of Capricorn runs through Queensland.

13 The black box is an Australian invention

14 April

15 Sir Charles Kingsford Smith

UNIT 5 First people

Grammar

pages 26–28

1 **a** S **b** P **c** S **d** P **e** S

2 **a** Some rock paintings in the West Australian Kimberleys are millennia old.

b Yagan was a warrior who lived and fought for his land in Western Australia.

c Rock paintings in the bush around Sydney depict the traditional life of local people.

d The poet, Oodgeroo Noonuccal, lived for most of her life on Stradbroke Island.

e It is difficult to survive in the arid western desert districts of Australia.

3 Jandamarra, a fearless Aboriginal warrior, decided he would not allow Europeans to take over his people's land in the Kimberleys as had happened down south. Here, **on his people's land**, he took a stand against the continuing land hunger of the white man. **For three years**, he carried on his fight to prevent his land, the land **of the Bunuba people**, being cleared for cattle grazing. Without their land his people could not live **in their old ways** by hunting, fishing and gathering roots **from the ground** and berries **from the bush**. Jandamarra was killed in his war but his memory lives on **in the hearts** of his people.

4 **b** played
c painted
d was elected
e was recognised
f toured
g played
h was

5 **b** signs
c work
d reputation
e People

6 **b** Aborigines used to set stone traps ✗ in rivers to catch eels.

c Inuit can build houses ✗ out of blocks of ice in one or two hours.

d Cathy Freeman ran ✗ for Australia in two Olympic Games.

e Many ancient sketches have been found ✗ on cave walls in desert regions.

f Storytelling ✗ by elders is a feature of every race and culture.

7 When we visited our cousins in the Northern Territory, they took us to a long sandy

beach where two men with long spears were spearing fish. It looked easy, so I found a long thin branch and carefully whittled a stabbing point with my pocketknife. I waded in and looked about for a fish but I couldn't see one. Meanwhile, the Aboriginal men had already caught five by my count. Finally, a small fish flashed past my knee. I hurled my spear and plunged into the water to retrieve my catch. But there was no fish and my spear bobbed lazily on the surface.

Just then a brown arm scooped me out of the water. 'Didn't you see that croc eyeing you off for dinner, little mate?' The tall man grinned as he pointed to the telltale swish of a croc tail in the water. 'Come away from the water, and I'll show you how to make a real throwing spear while we wait till he goes away.'

8 The Aboriginal flag is two bands of colour, red and black with a round gold sun in the middle of the banner.

Punctuation pages 29–30

1
- **a** What hunting weapons were used by Indigenous Australians in the past?
- **b** I wonder how people learned to find water under the desert.
- **c** Get out ! There's a crocodile right behind you.
- **d** The area around Lake Mungo is all Barkindji country.
- **e** Would I catch snakes? Not on your life! If I leave them be, they'll leave me be too.

2 Teacher: Who knows how places get their names?

Lionel: My Dad says that some places have Aboriginal names that tell what happened there or what it looked like.

Teacher: That's right, Lionel. Parramatta actually means a place where eels lie down.

Matt: *(beating his desk top with his fist)* We are the Eels! We are the Eels!

Teacher: Yes, we all know how you love your football team, Matt.

Alisha: I read somewhere that Katoomba means a place of falling water.

Denton: An old man told me that Gerringong, where we go for holidays, means a place of peril.

Teacher: Goodness me! I won't be holidaying there if that's the case.

3 **a** . **b** ! **c** ? **d** . **e** .

4 **a** ? **b** ? **c** . **d** ? **e** .

5 How do you think you would fare in the Wild Dog Range for three whole days? Two thirteen-year-olds from Smithtown recently had the chance to find this out. Searchers had almost given up hope of finding them when they heard the cry: Smoke! I can see smoke.

Within ten minutes James Henderson and Peter Vella had been winched to safety by helicopter. Reporters met them at the airport. One asked how they came to be found so far from their planned route.

When the boys told of losing their compass and taking a wrong turn up a gully, they were asked how they lost it. The boys confessed that a possum had run up a tree with it and that neither of them was any good at climbing trees. An unheroic end to a great survival tale! Well done, boys. (OR An unheroic end to a great survival tale. Well done, boys!)

6
- **a** Jim Jackson, a Year 8 student, mounted a display of Indigenous Australian books and music CDs.
- **b** What a throw! The boomerang flew twenty metres and even disappeared over the hills for a second. It then curved back and flew directly into the hands of the thrower.
- **c** In 2008 the Australian Prime Minister formally apologised to Indigenous Australian people for past wrongs.

UNIT 6 Our region

Grammar pages 31–34

1 **a** and **b** but **c** and **d** if **e** because **f** Whenever **g** When

2 **a** and **b** and **c** but **d** but **e** and **f** but **g** nor **h** or

3 **a** but **b** although **c** and **d** and then **e** although **f** until

4 **a** when **b** if **c** and **d** but **e** but **f** Although

5 When we set out on our trek into the jungle we were excited but we had no idea what the day would bring. Our elephant swayed constantly from side to side so we all felt sick. Although we had covered ourselves with Aerogard, we were eaten alive by mozzies. A monkey stole my hat, and then he snatched Ingrid's biscuits and ran up a tree with them. When we stopped to look at a waterfall, a spider fell onto Ingrid's shoulder. This made her scream so the elephant trumpeted loudly in fright.

6
- **a** China's biggest river is the Yangtze **but** it has several other great rivers too.
- **b** I won't go to the crocodile display **because** I am frightened of crocodiles.
- **c** **If** it does not rain we will go to the night markets.
- **d** You aren't able to come with me **so** I won't go to the night markets this evening.
- **e** Don't go out in the sun **unless** you wear a very large hat.
- **f** **While** we visited the temple, Dad went on a long bush trek.

7
- **a** Asian pythons are as thick as your arm and very long **but** they are not venomous **and** they only hunt small creatures.
- **b** The last days of the dry season are terribly hot **but then** (OR **and then**) it rains **and** suddenly the air is cool and fresh.
- **c** The sun's rays come down vertically at the Equator **so** it is always hot there **and** there is no summer or winter. OR **Because** the sun's rays come down vertically at the Equator, it is always hot there **and** there is no summer or winter.

8
- **a** so, as
- **b** when, so
- **c** Because, and
- **d** Although, so
- **e** Unless, because

9
- **a** because **b** Although **c** when/if
- **d** unless **e** if

10 **Incorrect**: because (should be deleted; no conjunction is needed but a semicolon should be added)
whenever (should be *wherever*)
although (should be *and*)
because (should be *when* or *if*)

Punctuation pages 35–36

1
- **a** Singapore, an island and a city in one, is the most modern city in southern Asia.
- **b** Fiji, and northern Fiji in particular, has spectacular rainforests that can be explored with the help of a guide.
- **c** The Indian cobra, one of the world's most venomous snakes, can inflate a threatening hood on its head.
- **d** The zookeeper and his assistant, hot in pursuit of the escaped monkeys, cried out for help.
- **e** A newcomer to Shanghai, the Pearl of the Orient, could be excused for being overwhelmed by its 24/7 way of life.
- **f** The Hibiscus Festival, a week-long event popular with Fiji locals and tourists alike, takes place in the first week of August with parades, music and fireworks.

2
- **a** The Diwali Festival marks the beginning of the Hindu New Year, and so many Indian businesses start a new accounting year on the Diwali Festival date.
- **b** The main language spoken in Fiji is English, but most locals speak the Fijian language or Hindustani as well.
- **c** Ramadan is the ninth month of the Muslim calendar year, and, during this time, Muslim people do not eat or drink during daylight.
- **d** Last year our school had a small multicultural day, but this year we are joining with two other schools to have a combined multicultural festival.

3
- **a** ii ✔
- **b** i ✔
- **c** ii ✔

4
- **a** During the summer, days become longer and longer.
- **b** For Jenny, Thomas would always be a champion.
- **c** Soon after, the concert began.

5
- **a** ✔
- **b** ✘
- **c** ✔
- **d** ✘

6 Indonesia, that volcanic chain of islands stretching from Northern Sumatra to West Irian's border with Papua New Guinea, is home to people of many different ethnic groups. These include the Minangkabau of Sumatra, the Javanese, the Balinese, the Madurese and the Dayaks of Sabah. Although in the past they all spoke different languages, everyone now speaks the national language Bahasa Indonesia, and so communication across the islands is easier.

UNIT 7

Wrecks and other calamities

Grammar pages 38–39

1 **a** present **b** past **c** future
d present **e** past

2 **a** The whale surfaced and spouted water from its vent.

b Divers always wear pressure suits when they are diving.

c In polar regions ships' crews fear iceberg contact.

d Badly loaded cargo sank a small ship.

e Great tankers will load tonnes of oil at terminals in the Middle East.

3 **a** caused **b** were **c** goes **d** exploded

4 **a** were battling

b are hauling

c were dragging

d are lifting

e are taking

5 Bushfires are part of every Australian's experience. They **are** not confined just to the bush. Heat, wind and lack of rain **raise** the risk of fire to Extreme in any location, especially when there **is** plenty of dry grass around. It **takes** only seconds for a fire to take hold when these conditions are present. A cigarette butt, a spark from a barbecue or a flash of lightning **starts** a fire in a flash.

6 **a** The wind **howls/is howling** and there **is** no moon.

b Lighthouse signals **are** visible in the dark.

c The freighter's engines **are failing** under the weight of the stormy sea.

d At a frightening speed the ship **surges** towards the cliff and **breaks** up.

e Many sailors **dream** of circumnavigating the globe alone.

7 **a** past **b** present **c** past **d** future
e past **f** present

8 I will write an essay on the wreck of the *Batavia*. I will have a book from the library about the wreck so I will be able to get the facts straight before I write.

Punctuation pages 40–41

1 **a** 'Gulliver's Travels'

b 'Jurassic Park'

c 'Cats'

d 'Advance Australia Fair'

e 'Sesame Street'

2 Our library has just acquired a large batch of new books and magazines. There are the latest 'Street Cars' and 'All Terrain Vehicle' magazines for the auto enthusiasts as well as a CD in the back of 'Street Cars' for all the great street car sound effects. There's even a great new Kawasaki manual with cross-section diagrams called 'Off-Road Racing'.

3 **a** ✗

b ✓

c ✗

d ✓

e ✓

4 Mr James wanted everyone present including cast, lighting people and prompts. I didn't think I wanted to see Shakespeare's play, 'Hamlet', on stage on such a hot sticky day but it was worth it to see Ben play Hamlet and leap about the stage in tights. Oscar was reading Tim Winton's 'Blue Boy' and missed it all, even the bit where Ben talked to a skull, so of course he doesn't understand why Ben's new nickname is 'Skull'.

5 **a** Mr Swan said these were easy, so how come these 'easy' maths questions are so hard to do?

b My mates all go by their own names except Tom, who prefers his nickname, 'Fitzie'.

c Shelve all the A-title books over there, starting with 'Arthur the Aardvark'.

d Grandfather used to sing a great little song called 'My Marvellous Toy.' Did you ever hear it?

e Some people prefer 'pie-in-your-face' humour to clever, witty dialogue.

6 a David is listening to rap music and watching 'The Hunger Games' at the same time.

b That documentary's soundtrack sounds like one called 'The Flight of the Condor'.

c It's only a 'fine' day if you're a penguin; it's cold and wet out there.

d Have you read 'The Count of Monte Cristo'? I haven't, but I have seen the DVD.

e Every age has its 'in' word, a word everyone uses for six months, then forgets again.

7 False—Smiths Crisps is a brand, not a title.

UNIT 8 Out in space

Grammar pages 43–44

1 a Our sun
b The white-tiled space shuttle
c The first lunar landing team
d the whole space crew
e China

2 a revolves b circle c believes
d are e does f has

3 a have b was c is d have e are

4 a rotate b shines c burns
d twinkle e is

5 a ✗
c ✗

6 a is unique to the Southern Hemisphere.
b are also constellations in space.
c circles the planet Neptune.
d lasts only eighty-eight days.
e are from one to three eclipses.

7 Comets **blaze** a trail of fire across the night sky. Some comets **have** a long life so they reappear regularly. Halley's Comet **comes** around every 76 years and will next be seen in 2061. The Hale-Bopp comet **was** last seen in 1995 and will not **be** around for another 2 365 years. At present astronomers **list** almost 1000 comets, but there are several thousand in our solar system which **remain** unseen.

8 are, travel, collect, know, are, runs, proceed, think, are

9 is, does, breathe, survive, are

Punctuation pages 45–47

1 a RAAF b CSIRO c MP
d PC e 4WD f EST

2 a ASIO b QANTAS c NATO
d LASER e ANZAC f SCUBA

3 a LAWS b GASS c FIGS d MAMA

4 a Mt Kosciusko
b Fairy Hole Rd
c Vic. or VIC
d Smith St
e Whitlam Cres.
f Murrumbidgee Ave

5 a company b sergeant
c junior d digital video (or versatile) disc
e department f established
g point h Short Message Service

6 Jan., Feb., Apr., Aug., Sept., Oct., Nov., Dec.

7 a ✓
b ✗
c ✗
d ✗
e ✓

8 Answers will vary.

9 Mt Misery, Henley Blvd, Long Point Dr., Medivac, iPhone, SOS, Patrick Bros

Revision Test 2

Grammar pages 48–50

1 near, on, after, in, beside, to

2 around

3 in the east

4 walking on the moon was once sheer imagination.

5 when, so, and, unless, because

6 and

7 but

8 when

9 Volcanoes in Java are erupting right now.

10 will sing

11 is

12 has

13 lived

14 Kai went swimming yesterday and will swim again next Friday.

15 will be

16 The football team in red won all their matches.

17 Each of the elephants is enjoying its bath in the river.

Punctuation pages 50–51

1 ?

2 Which planet is closer to the sun, Mercury or Venus?

3 I wonder if Darwin's wet season will come early this year.

4 Why is it hottest at the Equator?

5 No two bushfires are the same or behave the same.

6 The trekkers wanted to get to the camp by nightfall, but they had to give up their goal because of heavy rain.

7 'Gulliver's Travels'

8 'Men in Black III'

9 'a sunburnt country'

10 Spinach, of course, is every child's 'favourite' vegetable.

11 'Up There, Cazaly' has become an AFL football anthem.

12 Mr and Mrs Jones lived in Japan for three years.

13 Who is the author of 'Storm Boy'?

UNIT 9 On the wings of fantasy

Grammar pages 53–55

1
- **a** ferocious, yapping
- **b** tabby, striped, friendly
- **c** placid, cranky
- **d** tall, shaggy, tethered
- **e** buzzing, vicious
- **f** cuddly, bleating

2 Adjectives of colour: snowy white, black, emerald.

Other adjectives: curled, gilded, ghostly, tall, long, little, cool, clear, silent

3 His cloak was coal black, his hat was charcoal and he carried a thin black cane. He was a creature from the shadow world, this strange fellow with his claw fingers, hawk nose and gravel voice.

4 **b** magic, furry **c** flickering **d** lazy
e fairy, tiny, flower **f** mythical, spiralled

5 **a** ice **b** treasure **c** magic
d swallow-tailed **e** Hairy evil-eyed

6

Simple	Comparative	Superlative
strange	stranger	strangest
odd	odder	**oddest**
weird	**weirder**	weirdest
agile	**more agile**	**most agile**
skilled	more skilled	**most skilled**
friendly	**friendlier**	friendliest
fearsome	**more fearsome**	**most fearsome**

7
a ugliest
b hardest
c most terrible
d most delicate
e most beautiful

8
a more outgoing
b more mischievous
c more colourful
d odder
e scarier

9 **a** worst **b)** best **c)** worse **d)** better **e)** good

10
a ✔
b ✘
c ✘
d ✔
e ✘
f ✘

Punctuation pages 56–57

1 **a** has not **b** does not **c** will not
d have not **e** They have **f** He had

2 **a** couldn't **b** would've **c** I've
d needn't **e** should've **f** They'd

3 I'll, That's, I've, There's, hasn't

4 **a** didn't **b** won't **c** haven't
d hasn't **e** he'd **f** shouldn't
g can't **h** don't **i** they've
j mustn't **k** doesn't **l** weren't

5 **a** Who's **b** Whose **c** Who's
d whose **e** Who's

6
a They're
b Their, their
c They're, they're
d their
e they're, they're

7
a its
b It's, It's, it's
c it's, it's
d It's
e its

8
a Where
b We're
c Where
d Where, Wear
e We're, We're, where

9
a is'nt, isn't
b hav'ent, haven't
c theyr'e, they're
d was'nt, wasn't
e dident, didn't
f does'nt, doesn't
g cats, cat's
h her's, hers
i arent', aren't

UNIT 10 Grand designs

Grammar pages 59–60

1
a usually shrouded
b gleams brightly
c cleverly linked
d slowly subsiding
e always provides

2 **a** sometimes **b** now **c** originally
d regularly **e** easily

3 **a** where **b** when **c** how
d how often **e** how often

4 It was quite tiring climbing the hill to the Tower, but when we got there the view was absolutely spectacular. We could see the Yangtze River winding slowly across the plain, the carefully tended farms and the city in the distance. However, it was the Yellow Crane Tower itself that I most enjoyed. I loved the highly polished timber floors and the balconies roofed over with yellow ceramic tiles. I loved its unexpectedly cool interior, the faintly whispering breeze under its curved eaves and, especially, the enormously tall red-lacquered pillars that have stood there for centuries.

5
- **a** **ii** That was terrific fun.
- **b** **ii** The team works together well.
- **c** **i** The building went up quickly.
- **d** **i** The climb is really hard.
- **e** **ii** Look really slowly and carefully.

6 See yourself lazily swimming among tropical fish? Bravely leaping off a cliff and bouncing back just before you hit the ground? Dining romantically in the moonlight? Book now—six glorious days on your very own tropical island for a mere $900.

7 While I was waiting to climb the Sydney Harbour Bridge, I was rather scared and was very glad my elder brother had come with me. He's an engineering student and knows quite a lot about bridge construction. If he kept talking while we were climbing, I might not look down and see the green water far below. Soon we were on our way. It was a long way to the top and I started to puff halfway but it was well worth the climb. The view from the arch was spectacular.

8
- **a** tomorrow **b** yesterday
- **c** today **d** tonight

Punctuation pages 61–62

1
- **a** 'Who designed the Eiffel Tower in Paris?' asked Selma.
- **b** 'Did you know that London Bridge was demolished and rebuilt in America?' Sam inquired.
- **c** 'What sort of road machine does your father drive?' asked Peter.
- **d** 'Did you visit the Red Fort in Delhi when you were there?' Mrs Harris enquired.
- **e** The tourist guide warned us: 'Don't enter the roped off areas of the castle.'

2
- **a** 'I love medieval castles,' Maria told her father.
- **b** 'How did people raise the giant statues on Easter Island?' asked the student.
- **c** The overseer shouted 'Pull!' and the workers hauled on the rope.
- **d** 'Jim drives huge ore trucks at the iron mine,' his brother said proudly.
- **e** 'Good grief!' Mrs Bindon exclaimed at the sight of the mud on their work clothes.

3
- **a** 'What is this Taj we're supposed to be discussing?' David wanted to know. 'I've been away all week and I don't know what we're talking about.'
- **b** 'It's a mausoleum, a big above-ground tomb, in India,'offered Lal.
- **c** 'And it's a memorial too,' chimed in Jai. 'The Emperor Shah Jehan built it to honour his wife.'
- **d** 'He must have loved her very much,' sighed Amy. 'Is it a very beautiful memorial?'
- **e** 'Tomorrow we'll be talking about the ruins of Petra,' said Mrs Hadad. 'Please read up and come prepared.'

4 ['How did people warm those old European castles?' Fiona asked her history teacher. 'If they were built of stone they must have been very cold in winter.' ['Yes they were, Fiona. That's a good question. Can anyone tell us how they were heated?' ['I know, Sir,' Tom called out. 'They built a great big fire in every room.' ['But there were lots and lots of rooms,'objected William.

5
- **a** true **b** false **c** true
- **d** true **e** false

6
- **a** A reference book, 'Bridge Construction', lay on a table. 'Would you put it back on its shelf please, Elizabeth?' the librarian said.
- **b** The girls hired a movie called 'The Matrix', only to have Tom say, 'I've seen that.'
- **c** The protesters waved two kinds of banners, one saying 'Save our wilderness' and the other 'No more dams!'

d Peter read the sign aloud: 'No object shall be thrown from this bridge. Penalty for infringement $280.'

e 'Haul away!' the groundsman shouted to the crane driver. 'The load's secure.'

7 a 'Are you going to the new indoor pool?' Colin asked us.

b 'What is the likely completion date?' inquired Head Office.

c 'The usual pagoda colours in China are red, green and gold,' Hong Liu told us.

d 'All modern buildings use reinforced concrete,' the architect reassured Mr Habib.

UNIT 11 Having fun

Grammar pages 63–65

1 a goes walking

b climbed

c cycles, runs, swims

d thinks, makes

2 a S b C c S
d C e S

3 a Irene enjoys sewing and she especially enjoys embroidery.

b Paul collects foreign stamps but Charlie and Craig collect football cards.

c The girls played hard until the final whistle but they were beaten in the end.

d Acting appeals to many people but Heidi wanted to be theatrical lighting engineer.

e As a child Henry watched butterflies, then he graduated to collecting them and finally he became an entomologist with butterfly expertise.

f Penny learned to knit but that was not enough for her and she learned to crochet too.

4 a Archery looks easy **but** it takes tremendous strength to draw back the bow.

b Long boards were once popular **but** modern short boards are better for surfing.

c Sharks swim close to the shore in summer **so** wise surfers stay behind the shark net.

d My mother was not keen on my playing football **and/so** she suggested I play cricket or tennis.

e The Browns Flat team were bigger **but** our team was faster **so** we won.

f Do you like doing extreme sports **or** do you prefer to watch them on TV?

5 a but b but c but
d or e or

6 but, and, but, or

7 The table game of Mahjong began in China. It is played with a set of 136 small rectangular tiles. Each tile carries a symbol or a Chinese writing character. Four players each draw 13 tiles. The object of the game is to build a city wall with these tiles. The player who first exhausts the supply of tiles wins.

The best sentences to join are:

It is played with a set of 136 small rectangular tiles and each tile carries a symbol or a Chinese writing character.

The object of the game is to build a city wall with these tiles and the player who first exhausts the supply of tiles wins.

8 Here is one answer:
Surfing is the greatest fun. You paddle out, you turn and you wait for a big wave to roll in. You catch it, then straighten out balancing your feet fore and aft, and ride your wave in. If you're lucky it will curl over you so you can ride across the underbelly of the wave inside the curl of its crest.

9 a (but), so

b (because), but

Punctuation pages 66–67

1 b in Dr Hale's laboratory

c in the girls' class

d with many people's support

e in the ocean's black depths

f in the men's race

2 a fencer's b diver's c car's
d Canada's e rowers' f swimmers'

3 a (no) b (yes) c (yes)
d (yes) e (no)

4 cage's, Marcie's, boys', Dad's, Mr Harris's/Mr Harris', shed's

5 **a** Men's **b** Chris's/Chris' **c** rink's
d girls' **e** choir's

6 **a** ✗
b ✗
d ✗
f ✗
g ✗

UNIT 12 A world of colour

Grammar pages 69–70

1 **a** which is a highly visible colour.
b because it is going to rain.
c although I missed the first bus.
d whenever she has time.
e who was to lead our bush excursion
f who must protect their young
g when viewed underwater

2 **a** which **b** that **c** whose
d where **e** when

3 **a** when autumn closes in
b as Namatjira's painting show
c where wild creatures roam in vast herds
d which lie west of Sydney
e which run down to the shores of the blue Aegean

4 No correct answers, but here are some examples:
b When she went sailing
c before they went for a swim.
d When you look down from the mountain
e If you want to be a rock-climber
f as we set up camp.

5 No correct answers, but here are some examples.
b which is a great red desert rock
c that led into the forest.
d that swept in from the north.
e that/which twinkled like diamonds.

6 **a** S **b** D **c** D **d** D **e** S

7 Quartz-spark stars catch the light of a pale moon like the tiny mirrors that gleam from Indian veiling. The Southern Cross shines cold as glass, as it did when the Nunnawal first sang its Dreamtime story to wide-eyed children.

8 Outside my room a gum tree stands **where** it has stood for at least a hundred years. It is taller than the chimney of our house **and** is at least three metres around its trunk. Its bark, **which** cracks and peels off every autumn, reveals new silver-white bark. Over the year this new bark turns various colours from pink through to grey. **When** it rains the bark shines pink, grey, yellow, green and mauve **so** it almost looks like a painting.

Punctuation pages 71–72

1 **a** When the sun sets over the horizon,
b Because the sloth has bad hearing and bad sight,
c Although the toucan's large yellow bill looks frightening to predators,
d While the clownfish might look pretty with its orange and white stripes,
e When a bee finds flowers with nectar,

2 **a** , which we think of as yellow,
b , which is usually white,
c , after high tide has washed it clean,
d , which grows in cool misty valleys,
e , after a storm has raged through,

3 **a** ✗
b ✓
c ✗
d ✓
e ✓

4 Dear Nathan,

We are here in my grandmother's village, where all my ancestors have lived for generations and I'm having a ball. Uncle Pham, who's my Dad's oldest brother, takes me fishing out on Halong Bay every morning. We row out at first light and drop our lines near one of the islands. Quickly we catch enough fish for breakfast and hurry home. If we're really lucky, Grandma will be waiting to grill them up for us. It will be good to get back home to catch up with what's been happening while I've been away, but I'll never forget this trip.

5 In our back garden, which is very steep, ✗ and has lots of rockeries, I have a pet blue-tongued lizard. He's not really a pet, I know, but he behaves like one. He's about as long as a ruler, and quite fat. His tongue really is blue, as his name suggests, and his eyes are bright black, ✗ and curious. His body is striped, ✗ vividly, ✗ in yellow and brown, although most other blue tongues, ✗ I have seen, ✗ are shades of blue grey. He lives in a crevice, but, ✗ he sleeps on top of a boulder, ✗ during the day if the sun is out.

6 **a** precise, **b** goes, travels, **c** Bluey, parents, **d** sea, **e** dowdy, **f** snakes, creatures **g** Quolls, carnivores, wallabies, small

Revision Test 3

Grammar pages 73–75

1 large, tiny, purple, heavy, unexpected

2 The Eiffel Tower is the tallest building in Paris.

3 Tracey was the worst cyclone to strike Australia.

4 Eddie is more careful than Tom.

5 Shelley was really careful.

6 The boys completed the task quickly.

7 originally

8 here, anxiously, silently, really, always

9 but

10 because

11 unless

12 If

13 three

14 two

15 The great river slowly made its winding way to the sea.

16 The weird Min Min light can be frightening when it is first encountered.

Punctuation pages 75–76

1 isn't

2 weren't

3 haven't

4 should've

5 theirs

6 Harvey's house plan

7 'Stop, drop and crawl,' said the fireman when he told the children about fire safety.

8 'We could have won,' said Kyle. 'What do you think, Joe?'

9 'In which state is the Westgate Bridge?' asked James.

10 Penny Lewis's house is built of mud bricks.

11 My next door neighbours have just moved to Queensland.

12 Both boys' tents were damaged by the hailstorm.

13 Before the girls started on their long trek, they left all their trip details with the police.

14 Hannah Gilmore, who knows a lot about gardening, reckons I should plant a lemon tree.

15 If you really want to go out, take a raincoat.

16 first,

UNIT 13 Ambitions and adventures

Grammar pages 78–79

1
- **a** Kai—will, the only thing
- **b** Dan—Not sure, I guess I could, maybe

2
- **a** might, would
- **b** can, can
- **c** must, can, can
- **d** should
- **e** can, must definitely

3 **a** **i** H must

ii L I think, need to

b **i** L may

ii H must

c **i** H will

ii L Perhaps, could

d **i** L could possibly

ii H ought

e **i** H have to

ii L should, probably

4 **a** 2 **b** 4 **c** 3
d 1 **e** 5

5 **a** **ii** Team meeting 11 am. Please bring your gear with you. Your punctuality would be appreciated.

b **i** I don't think it was such a good idea to tell Carey.

c **ii** Could you let me know if you think you might be interested?

6 We went caving at the weekend. Once inside the cave, we followed a small underground stream into a large chamber that looked as if it **could**/**may**/**might** have once been the reception hall of a king. As we looked around we **could** hear a rustling above our heads. It **could**/**may**/**might** have been bats but we **will** never know because we fled back until it was **possible** to see the clean blue sky above. My father thinks it was **probably** just a drift of leaves on ledges near the roof of the cave, but the **possibility** of bats flapping round us in the dark **may**/**might**/**could** well see us taking up abseiling instead.

7 **a** High modality:
All band members must attend Eisteddford practice n Monday, Wednesday and Friday after school. Attendance all day Saturday is compulsory. Band members must bring their own lunch as well as their instrument.

b Low modality:
We'll be practising for the Eisteddford on Monday, Wednesday and Friday after school and all day Saturday. It would be good if all bands people could be there. And don't forget to bring your lunch as well as your instrument on Saturday or you might be very hungry.

Punctuation pages 80–81

1 **a** (33.6 feet)

b (also called dune busting)

c (one of the more extreme sports)

d (flying without power)

e (usually an aeroplane)

f (fighting with slim swords called foils)

g (global positioning system)

2 **a** —don't just pat the ball—

b —and a very good one—

c —mmm, just smell that exhaust.

d —ouch—

e —not to mention luck—

f —silly boy—

3 **a** On our Year 8 school camp we did all sorts of adventurous things. One thing we did—the best thing we did—was build a flying fox. Our camp supervisor—take a bow, Mr Loukakis—told us what to do and we built it ourselves. When it was finished we all had a turn flying between the trees at either end. We built it over a waterhole so some of us accidentally—like on purpose accidentally—fell from the ropes into the water. It was great fun.

b Dashes are suited to this text because it is written in an informal style.

4 **a** ✔

b ✔

c ✗

d ✗

e ✗

f ✔

5 Elise clung to the cliff. She had to swallow the taste of fear as she stretched upwards to a small hole that could serve as her next climbing grip. Spiders liked little holes too and she heaven help her was scared witless of spiders. Fortunately the hole was unoccupied. Elise gripped firmly with her right hand, then wedged her left foot into a narrow rock chimney that miraculously ran all the way to the cliff top. She looked upwards and saw no, surely it wasn't possible her faithful little dog, Patch. Now she knew she would be OK.

UNIT 14 Heroes and heroines

Grammar pages 82–84

1 **b** **i** A
ii P
c **i** A
ii P
d **i** P
ii A
e **i** A
ii P
f **i** P
ii A

2 **b** were saved—passive
c are attended—passive
d established—active
e were pulled—passive
f was awarded—passive

3 **a** are fought
b were assisted
c were rescued
d was treated
e was cut out

4 **b** The principle of non-violence was taught by Mahatma Ghandi.
c Slavery in the United States was abolished in 1863 by President Abraham Lincoln.
d Working girls in early New South Wales were protected by Caroline Chisholm.
e The first computer was invented by an Englishman, Charles Babbage.

5 1st passive:
the driver was trapped. The passive verb is suitable—it is not necessary or possible to say what he was trapped by—it is the fact that he is trapped that is important.

2nd passive:
was seen arriving. The passive verb is unsuitable because it slows the pace of the text, and does not fit the rest of the text which focuses on the main people. It would be better to write *We saw the ambulance arriving minutes later.*

6 Eddie Koiki Mabo was born in 1936 in the Murray Islands of the Torres Straits. Eddie **fought** for his people's ownership of their Murray Islands to **be recognised** by the Courts of Australia. The battle **was waged** peacefully in meetings, the media and the courts. In 1992 the High Court of Australia **decided** that title to the Murray Islands belonged to the people of the Murray Islands, Eddie Mabo's people. Sadly, Eddie **did not live** to hear this decision, dying five months before it **was handed down** by the Court.

7 **was invented**, **were freed**, **be sewn**, **took**

Punctuation pages 85–86

1 **a** 'Did you know that three men have won two Victoria Crosses each?' asked Tom.
b 'No, I didn't. Tell me about them,' his brother replied.
c 'Firefighters are the bravest people I know,' Geordie declared.
d 'Sailors who climbed masts to set sails must have been very brave,' Elizabeth told her history class.
e Peter looked up from his book to say, 'My sister is a surf lifesaver. You can't get any braver than that.'

2 **a** Rosemary asked if anyone knew what really happened to the pilot, Amelia Erhart.
b 'Hey, you in the red jumper! That's not fair play,' the referee shouted.
c 'Construction workers on high-rise buildings must have nerves of steel,' Steve said.
d 'Why do magpies swoop in Springtime?' Fatima asked.
e Martha told Fatimah that magpies swoop to drive people away from babies in their nest.
f His father said that he should face his fears. 'But I'm only six years old,' the boy cried.

3 'Let's go climbing today,' Alex said. Everyone except William thought it a great idea. William's excuse was that he had chores to do. 'That's all right,' Alex said, 'We'll wait till you've done your chores. Then we'll go.' There was a pause, then William mumbled, 'I don't really have chores to do. I'm just scared of heights.' The others confessed that they had also been scared when they had first seen the climbing wall. Gino told him, 'You'll love it once you get used to it.' William looked doubtful but agreed that he would at least go and watch.

4
- **a** iii 'Go away!' he shouted.
- **b** i He wondered why he was late.
- **c** i The boys said that it had been a blast.
- **d** i The teacher asked if Joe had won.

5
- **a** i The doctor said he was a very lucky boy.
- **b** i The girl asked if he would help her.
- **c** ii The teacher asked what his real name was.
- **d** i The witness reported seeing a red car nearby.

UNIT 15 Mist and fog

Grammar pages 88–89

1

a	F	**b**	F	**c**	F	**d**	F
e	S	**f**	S	**g**	F	**h**	F
i	F	**j**	S				

2
- **a** Ducks on the river **paddled silently in the mist.**
- **b** Traffic, already heavy**, slowed to a crawl in the fog.**
- **c** Shafts of sunlight streaming through the mist **turned it gold.**
- **d** Settled over the surface of the reservoir **was a blanket of fog.**
- **e** It being already an hour after sunrise**, the mist was beginning to lift.**

3

a	When	**b**	As	**c**	While
d	Since	**e**	Unless	**f**	Until
g	If	**h**	Before	**i**	Because
j	Whether				

4
- **a** (ii) Craig, having a cold, was absent from training.
- **b** (i) Generally delayed by sea fog, the ferry is on time today.
- **c** (ii) Houses in England, a cold damp country, often have problems with rising damp.
- **d** (ii) She stood to one side thinking and drinking a hot chocolate.
- **e** (i) To create an eerie atmosphere, use a fog machine.

5 Contrary to popular belief/While mist rises from the ground/The expressions 'fog settling' and 'mist rising'

6
- **a** The waratah flourishes in a cold climate, thriving in deep wet mountain valleys.
- **b** Looking out, Callum spied an unknown figure in the mist striding purposefully towards the house.
- **c** It being confused by steam filling the bathroom, I walked into the door and broke my nose.
- **d** Although it was difficult in the circumstances, we all tried to remain hopeful.
- **e** Frost melting on the windows turned into rivulets down the glass, making puddles on the sill.

7 **a** & **d**

Fragments are suitable in **a** because it is an informal text and in **d** because it is a creative text.

Punctuation pages 90–91

1

a	S	**b**	R	**c**	R
d	S	**e**	R		

2
- **a** Ghost stories frighten me. They all feature dark nights and strange noises. I get totally spooked.
- **b** Where are you? I can't see you. I can't see anything at all.
- **c** The fog thinned as the sun rose high in the sky. The seals decided to sun themselves on ice floes.
- **d** The mountain was silent and everything was white when suddenly they heard a great roar. An avalanche swept past the skiers.
- **e** Lighthouses in Bass Strait have saved

many ships and their crews. Great storms wrack the Strait and fog regularly makes rocks and small islands invisible.

8 **a** The fog descended without warning. It covered the land like a blanket so that he did not know where he was.

b Pilots engage the autopilot when they fly through thick clouds where visibility is non-existent.

c As the Lady of the Lake rose out of the water through the trailing mists of night, Arthur caught sight of a magnificent sword in her hand.

UNIT 16

Mixed messages

Grammar pages 93–94

1 Possible answers:

a **i** The miner cut into a vein of gold.

ii The miner cut into a vein in his foot.

b **i** Mr Gill is a teacher from France.

ii Mr Gill is a teacher of French.

c **i** The new mouse is dead in his cage.

ii The new mouse for my computer is dead.

2 **a** Stolen Jewellery Found Near OR Beside Statue

b Man with Wooden Leg Attacked by Dog.

c After Twenty Years Brothers Reunited in Library

d Barefoot Child Bitten by Snake

e Red Tape Delays New Bridge Construction.

3 **a** A **b** C **c** A **d** C
e C **f** C **g** A

4 **a** **ii** The octopus kept one black eye on us as we swam underwater.

b **ii** A brown snake, woken suddenly from his nap, bit Jasper on the foot.

c **i** I want the cream cakes in that window.

d **ii** Vines scratched us with their thorns as we wandered through the bush.

e **ii** "Jai, your jeans are ripped," said Michael.

5 **a** Mrs Turner discussed with his teachers her son's problems.

b We used Mark's binoculars to see the man. OR We saw the man who was using Mark's binoculars.

c Her children know how to make lovely chocolate crackles.

d I'll hold the nail and you hit it with the hammer when I nod my head.

e He was from the bank and was tall with a craggy face.

f I saw a man with muttonchops whiskers on a bike.

g When Fergus was only four, his grandfather took him to an AFL match.

Punctuation pages 95–97

1 **a** **A**ustralian teams usually do well in international rowing**.**

b **W**here is the local skateboard park**?**

c **S**urfing lessons are held every **S**unday at **W**est **A**valon **S**urf **C**lub**.**

d **I**s **N**ew **Z**ealand beating **A**ustralia in the **W**orld **C**up**?**

e Hey**!** **W**e beat the **W**estern **R**edbacks**.**

2 **a** ship's **b** men's **c** Sailors'
d women's **e** boys' **f** competitors

3 **a** ✗ New Potatoes Today

b ✗ Today's Special—Minestrone soup

c ✗ Latest styles here today

d ✗ Footwear Specialists

e ✓ Children's haircuts $5 only!

f ✓ Chicken and Fries to go!

g ✗ All Your Petcare Needs Here

h ✗ Neptune's Haven

4 **a** **i** I haven't seen you here before.

b **i** We shouldn't swim after dark.

c **ii** They're my oranges.

d **ii** It's not compulsory to attend.

e **i** The dog shook its head.

f **i** We're losing.

g **i** Who's playing today?

h **ii** There were three boats.

5 Know what you want to say. Make sure **it's** logical then write it carefully, paying attention to grammar and using all necessary punctuation. If you do this **you're** going to be a good writer. You may even become a great writer and figure in the **lists** of the top bestsellers of our age.

6 a ✔ b ✔ c ✘ d ✘ e ✘

7 a won't b they're c it's d haven't e aren't

8 a It's raining in Queensland. All its rivers are in flood. All its residents are wet and it's only going to get worse.

b 'Is it true that snakes can swim?' Tom asked as he looked out at the floodwaters. 'Yes it's true, all right. There's a snake right there and it's swimming easily. I don't think it's lost its cool at all,' Mike answered.

Revision Test 4

Grammar pages 98–99

1 I will finish this by tonight.

2 I might go sailing if the sea is not too choppy.

3 must

4 I may go to Indonesia next year.

5 The policeman chased the thief.

6 The house at number 5 was demolished by bulldozers.

7 were persuaded

8 Most of our time was spent swimming.

9 A chill wind gusted through the open door.

10 Southern right whales leaping out of the water delighted tourists.

11 Michael, being frightened out of his wits, hid behind the steel door.

12 Kangaroos grazing over there beyond the trees.

13 Seals sunning themselves on the rocks below the cliff.

14 Experts say bus passengers should be belted.

15 Kyra told Bonnie she owed her a dollar.

16 If your sink has a leaking tap, replace it immediately.

17 had been locked

Punctuation pages 100–101

1 My neighbour (the one who's the skydiver) had a car accident yesterday.

2 (the study of birds)

3 Duncan asked where Mia had been.

4 We're having spinach pie for lunch—I hate spinach pie—with ice-cream for sweets.

5 He asked why the fence had been cut.

6 "My pigeon," he said "has flown two hundred miles and back."

7 Elise has red hair. She plays the violin. She's very clever.

8 Full stops go after:
concert. night. along. move. lights. fainted.

9 Are you wearing your hat?

10 Those tickets are theirs.

11 That house has lost its roof.

12 The tree lost its leaves.

13 Tomatoes for sale.

14 It's

15 Mrs Eddy asked for every girl's science book.

16 The puppies' tails all wagged in unison.

17 everyone's